Highland
Landforms

Highland Landforms

Robert Price

ABERDEEN UNIVERSITY PRESS
Member of Maxwell Macmillan Pergamon Publishing Corporation

Revised edition 1991
Aberdeen University Press

© Robert J Price 1991

First published 1976

All the illustrations in this book apart from those listed below were provided
by the author.

Figs. 1 & 2: Dept of Geography and Topographic Science, Glasgow University.
Fig. 7: British Geological Survey. **Fig. 29:** A. Gibb. **Fig. 30:** Aerofilms Ltd.
Fig. 35: A Bremner and H.I.D.B. **Fig. 49:** W. Ritchie.

British Library Cataloguing in Publication Data

Price, R J (Robert John)
Highland landforms. – Rev. ed.
1. Highland Region (Scotland). Landforms
I. Title
551.41094115

ISBN 0-08-041196-7

Printed in Great Britain by
AUP Aberdeen – a member of BPCC Ltd

Contents

List of Illustrations

Maps

Preface

I wrote a very brief Preface to the first edition of this book and am pleased to be given an opportunity to write again. Having since had many opportunities to *use* the book to help me understand more fully how particular areas in the Highlands and Islands came to be what they are, and what the limitations, difficulties and potentialities of these areas are for distinctive types of development I appreciate and value even more highly the knowledge and skills which Dr Robert Price has brought to the production of this book.

The shape of the land made Highland history in as much as the winning and holding of land by tribes or clans was a central feature of Celtic life. A distinctive language and culture developed and was protected from intrusive influences by distance, landforms and the sea. The difficulty which landform created for transport was very gradually overcome, with military needs rather than trading interests playing the larger part in that process. It is ironic that the post-Culloden (1746) intent to destroy the clan system and subjugate the highlanders very soon resulted in the Highlands becoming the best recruiting ground for the British army. Again, the limited employment opportunities dictated by the geological and geographical nature of the area provides a major explanation.

In the modern world those who live in the Highlands and Islands, and most of those who visit the area recognise it as a most valuable nature reserve, surviving close by to an essentially urban society, but again insulated from that society's capacity to wither and destroy nature by distance and the shape of the land. There should be no surprise far less resentment at the protective responses of local communities to what they fear as encroachments on this valued element in their lives. Having enjoyed the benefits of the mountain barriers, the turbulent rivers and the more turbulent seas, it is natural to wish to retain the advantages even after technology has breached these defences.

I hope that this book will increase interest in and knowledge of the unique features of the Scottish Highlands and Islands. Visually the area cannot but encourage a certain humility, and an understanding of the origins of the area adds to that feeling. Hugh MacDiarmid's poem 'On a Raised Beach' makes the point well:

> We must be humble. We are so easily baffled by appearances
> And do not realise that these stones are at one with the stars.
> It makes no difference to them whether they are high or low,
> Mountain peak or ocean floor, palace, or pigsty.
> There are plenty of ruined buildings in the world but no ruined stones.

KENNETH ALEXANDER

Foreword

The first edition of this book was the third book in the 'Highland Life Series' produced by the Highland's and Island's Development Board. In introducing the first edition of Highland Birds, the first book in this series, Sir James Mackay wrote that 'the aim of the series was to establish a useful and authoritative Highland library. The library will tell, in words and pictures, what the Highlands and Islands are and contain . . .'

The two volumes published on Highland Birds and Highland Animals certainly achieved this aim. However, they dealt with topics which are very familiar to the general public and which can be appreciated without an understanding of the scientific background to the evolution of each species. Birds and animals 'live and move and have their being' for all to enjoy. Although everyone can see landforms as they exist as a part of the total environment, an understanding of how they came to be as they are requires some understanding of the history of the earth and of the processes responsible for the development of landforms. As Sir James Mackay pointed out in his preface to Highland Birds, 'Accurate knowledge leads to understanding and interest, and interest can lead to all sorts of developments'. My hope is that what follows in this book will make landforms more interesting to anyone visiting the Highlands and Islands.

In the second half of the nineteenth century Scotland was a major centre for research in geology. The wide variety of rocks and landforms of various ages provided an excellent field laboratory for geologists. Two books, 'The Scenery of Scotland' by Archibald Geikie (1865) and 'The Great Ice Age' by James Geikie (1873), summarised the results of this early work for the general reader. The great explosion of scientific knowledge over the past 50 years has resulted in the publication of a great many scientific papers on the rocks and landforms of Scotland. Many of these papers are summarised in 'The Geology of Scotland' edited by Craig (1983), 'The Evolution of Scotland's Scenery' by J. B. Sissons (1967) and 'Scotland's Environment

During the Past 30,000 Years' by R. J. Price (1983).

I am most grateful to the Highland's and Island's Development Board for originally giving me the opportunity to write this book. In particular, Gordon Lyall, James Grassie and Calum Munro provided encouragement and constructive criticism.

As a result of a change of policy by the H.I.D.B. the 'Highland Life Series' was discontinued. I was therefore delighted when Colin MacLean of Aberdeen University Press suggested that a new edition should be published. To his successor as managing director of AUP, Colin Kirkwood, and his staff I am most grateful for their efficient production of this book.

I am very conscious of the many sweeping generalisations which are made in the text. Such generalisations are only possible because of the painstaking detailed work of many individuals. To all those who have worked and are working on the problems of the origins of Scottish landforms, I acknowledge a deep debt.

Although I am interested in landforms primarily to discover more about their origins, perhaps they are even more important to me as a part of the total environment, and as a stage upon which nearly all of man's activities are performed. The Highlands and Islands contain a great variety of landforms which it can be claimed are the very core of the region's personality. They can delight the eye as a part of the landscape, infuriate the engineer or planner, be a challenge to the mountaineer or a series of problems in the mind of the earth scientist.

R J PRICE

THE SHAPE OF THE LAND

Anyone travelling through the Highlands and Islands of Scotland soon becomes aware of the variety of landscapes this region has to offer. Any landscape is a mixture of natural and man-made phenomena. On the one hand, the coastline, hills and valleys are the product of natural processes working over thousands or even millions of years while, on the other hand, the work of man is clearly seen in the enclosed fields devoted to agriculture or the extensive plantations of the Forestry Commission. Man-made structures such as crofter's cottages, paved roads, bridges or hydro-electric projects all add to, or detract from, the landscapes of the Highlands. The changes brought about by man, although of considerable extent, are relatively recent changes and have only partly modified the landscapes which have been produced by natural processes.

A fundamental attribute of natural landscapes is the form of the land itself. The study of the shape of the land surface and the processes responsible for creating that shape is known as geomorphology. This science is primarily concerned with explaining the origin of landforms; this involves an examination of the materials which constitute landforms – the rocks – and of the sculpturing processes which have carved these rocks into the shapes we see on the earth's surface.

In a period when man has the capability of exploring the surface of the moon it is surprising how little we know about the surface of our own planet. Cartographers have been able to demonstrate the complexity of the coastline of the Highlands and Islands for some 200 years and their maps have now been confirmed by satellite photography. For the first time we can actually view, with the aid of a camera, a large part of Scotland at one time (*Fig. 1*). What can be learned from this image taken from an altitude of 570 miles (920 km)? Firstly, it is possible to differentiate between land and water.

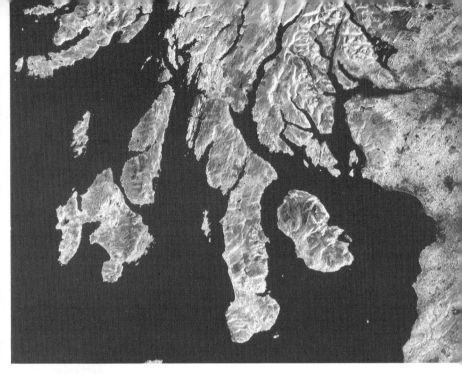

1. Satellite image of the South-West Highlands and the Firth of Clyde taken from an altitude of 570 mls (920km). The general shape of the coastline can be clearly seen along with some of the major geological structures, e.g. the Highland Boundary Fault.

The boundary between these two types of substance is the coastline and its highly indented character can be clearly seen. Why is this coastline so irregular and why are there so many small and some large fragments of land detached from the mainland? Details of the form of the land surface are difficult to see from this image. If we look at a photograph of a part of the Highlands taken from 10,000 feet (3,000 m), then much more detail can be seen (*Fig. 2*). The three corries on the north-west side of Cairngorm, the deep valley of Loch Avon and the magnificent trench of the Lairig Ghru can all be clearly seen. The summits of Cairngorm (4,084 feet, 1,225 m) and Ben Macdui (4,296 feet, 1,288 m) are not so easily recognised. To the expert many of the details of individual landforms, the nature of surface materials and structures in the solid rock can be interpreted from aerial photographs such as this. Nearly all the topographic maps of the Highlands and Islands are now produced from this type of aerial photography.

2. Aerial photograph of the Cairngorm Mountains.

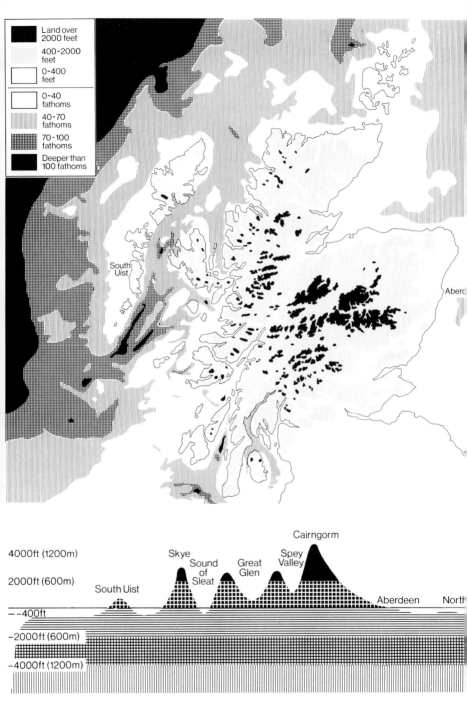

Land over 2000 feet

400-2000 feet

0-400 feet

0-40 fathoms

40-70 fathoms

70-100 fathoms

Deeper than 100 fathoms

South Uist

Aberd

Cairngorm

4000ft (1200m)

Skye

Spey Valley

2000ft (600m)

Sound of Sleat

Great Glen

South Uist

Aberdeen

Nortl

--400ft

-2000ft (600m)

-4000ft (1200m)

3. The distribution of land at various altitudes, and water depths on the continental shelf.

A great many maps at varying scales have been made of the land area of the Highlands and Islands and of the sea floor immediately adjacent to the Scottish coast. These maps provide a great deal of information about the altitude of the land area or the depth of water off the coast. These maps, if they have been contoured, also provide information about the shape of the land surface or the shape of the sea floor. When such maps are drawn at fairly large scales (1 : 100,000 or larger) they reveal some of the detailed shapes of the land or sea floor. It is questions about the origins of these shapes that we must try to answer.

A map showing the distribution of altitudes above and below sea level of that part of the globe with which we are concerned (*Fig. 3*) shows that some 60 miles (100 km) west of the Outer Hebrides water depths become much shallower, and that the Highlands and Islands represent the upstanding part of a shelf with a maximum altitudinal range of only about 5,000 feet (1,500 m).

Although this book will be primarily concerned with the form of the land areas some reference will be made to the form of the surface below the shallow seas. In terms of the origins of the coastline as well as of the increasing economic importance of off-shore areas, the nature of the continental shelf will be referred to from time to time.

The map of altitude distribution within the land area of the Highlands and Islands provides some general information about the nature of the landforms. Although the highest altitudes recorded are only a little over 4,000 feet (1,200 m) a very large percentage is between 1,000 feet (300 m) and 3,000 feet (900 m) above sea level, with only the extreme north-east of the mainland and parts of the Outer Hebrides and Orkney having any extensive areas below 500 feet (150 m). What the altitude map does not show is that the areas between 1,000 feet (300 m) and 3,000 feet (900 m) above sea level have very rapid changes in altitude and are characterized by steep slopes leading from valley floors to ridge tops. What are the causes of these variations in altitude and of the slope patterns associated with them?

Any landform is either the product of the sculpturing of the rocks of the earth's crust by weathering and erosion or of the accumulation of materials that have been eroded from one place and deposited in another. How the solid rocks of the earth's crust originate and are arranged at the surface will be discussed later, but let us examine now the processes which are responsible for

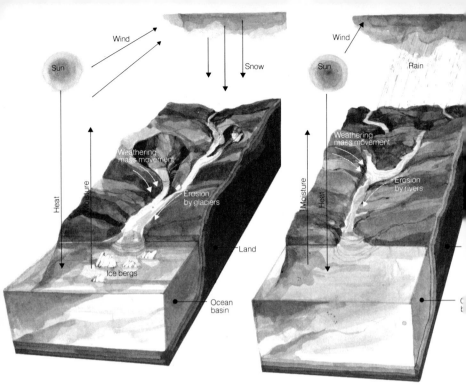

4. The 'geomorphological machine' is powered by energy from the sun. At present most of its work is accomplished by running water (rivers) and the breaking waves along the coast. In the recent geological past, in periods of cold climate, precipitation fell as snow which was transformed to ice glaciers).

weathering and eroding those rocks to create landforms.

Reference is often made to 'the everlasting hills'. Within the context of the human time scale it is reasonable to think of most hills, cliffs and mountain tops as unchanging. But in the context of geological time – which deals in thousands, millions and even hundreds of millions of years – the surface of the earth has undergone a great many changes. The concept of continental drift and sea-floor spreading has made us realise that the size, shape and position of land areas on our planet have changed greatly over hundreds of millions of years. Over millions of years any one part of the land area has also experienced great changes and is still being changed, albeit imperceptibly, by what we know as the 'geomorphological machine' (*Fig. 4*).

This machine derives its energy from the sun and the force of gravity. Heat from the sun causes water to be evaporated from the oceans; this is then carried as water vapour over the land areas by the wind systems. The water vapour is then released in the form of rain, which accumulates in the ground until there is sufficient water available to cut and maintain river channels. Water flows down these channels under the force of gravity and re-enters the oceans.

The water in the river channels erodes the floors and sides of the channels so that the channels are cut into the land surface, exposing new land surfaces for attack by weathering. Weathering consists of a series of processes which result in the breakdown of solid rock to produce a skin of loose rock fragments which creep down steep slopes under the force of gravity or are washed towards stream channels by excess surface water. The weathering processes are a very important part of the geomorphological machine as they make it easier for solid rocks to be eroded by flowing water, moving ice or the wind.

When the moisture falls over the land as snow instead of rain, the geomorphological machine becomes a different model. The snow is transformed into ice and, instead of rivers eroding their channels and carrying away weathered rock, great rivers of ice develop, which, although they move more slowly than running water, still move downhill under the force of gravity and are capable of a great deal of erosion.

Whether erosion is accomplished by flowing water or moving ice, the material is eroded from one location, carried by the water or ice and then deposited. A great deal of eroded material is carried away from the land areas and deposited on the ocean floors where it begins to form new rocks. Some of the eroded material is deposited on the land, particularly on the flood plains of river valleys, as deltas along the coast or, in the case of glacier activity, it leads to the development of new constructional landforms.

Reference has been made to the wind systems which carry moisture from the oceans on to the land. These winds also help to drive the geomorphological machine because the friction between the moving air and the water surface results in the development of waves. When these waves arrive at a shoreline they, too, attack and erode the land; part of the geomorphological machine is, therefore, responsible for shaping the detailed form of coastlines.

The various processes which erode the land produce distinctive landforms. Land which has been primarily sculptured by running water looks quite different from that primarily eroded by glaciers or waves. Variations in the rock types and rock structures being eroded can also produce different types of landforms. The net result of erosion by the geomorphological machine is the lowering of the land area but, depending on the nature of the rocks forming the land area, some parts of it may be more easily eroded than others. The nature of the rock type found at the surface on any land area is very much a function of the geological history of that area. It will be necessary to look at the main events in geological history and the resultant distribution of rock types and structures before examining the landforms of the Highlands and Islands.

One further complication in the operation of the geomorphological machine must be considered. Since solar radiation is the main source of energy which drives this machine, the climatic conditions in which the machine operates will be of great importance. In humid temperate environments rain will be plentiful and river action will be dominant. In polar or high altitude locations snow will occur and glacier action will be more important than river action. On this basis each of the major climatic regions of the world should have its own distinctive set of geomorphological processes and resultant landforms. This would be the case if climatic conditions had remained the same throughout geological time. But this has not been so. Even over the last three million years there have been dramatic changes of climate in Scotland. Moist temperate conditions similar to and much warmer than today have alternated with periods of extreme cold allowing the build up of great glaciers and ice-sheets.

If one examines the last 50 million years there clearly have been many other climatic conditions which have affected the operation of the geomorphological machine. Because of climatic fluctuations, an individual landform may well have evolved as a result of several different sets of processes. Unravelling the relative importance of these various processes in fashioning the landforms visible today, is what makes the study of landforms both fascinating and frustrating.

This is a brief introduction to the operation of the geomorphological machine. It is now necessary to look at the raw materials on which the machine works – the rocks. Then we will examine the two main models of the machine which have been at work in Scotland – the work of rivers and the work of ice. Putting the raw materials and the processes acting on them together, it will then be possible to look at certain examples of landform assemblages in the Highlands and Islands which give distinctive landscape characteristics. Finally, we will examine landforms in the broader context of the natural environment and evaluate them as natural resources.

THE ROCKS AND THEIR HISTORY

The arrangement of the different types of rock which constitute the surface of the earth has been brought about over very long periods of time. Our planet has existed for some 4,500 million years and only recently have we obtained a limited understanding of the development of the continental masses and ocean basins. The evidence used by geologists to reconstruct the history of the planet consists of the information revealed by the rocks which outcrop on the surface combined with borehole information and data derived from seismic information. Each of the continental land areas contains three types of rock: igneous, sedimentary and metamorphic. Igneous rocks solidify from a molten material known as magma. This magma originates at great depths beneath the earth's surface; great internal pressures force it to penetrate the solid, brittle, outer crust of the earth. Magma which solidifies before reaching the earth's surface is known as intrusive igneous rock (e.g. granite), whereas magma which pours out on to the earth's surface before solidifying is known as extrusive igneous rock (e.g. basalt).

Sedimentary rocks are composed of particles eroded from previously existing rock and transported to and deposited at a new location by running water, moving ice or the wind. The actual method of transportation and the environment in which deposition takes place gives the new sediment distinctive characteristics. Most sedimentary rocks exhibit some degree of sorting and stratification. That is, the clay, sand and gravel particles – which are the main constituents of all sedimentary rocks – are separated out during transportation and deposition to produce distinct layers or strata. When sedimentary rocks are originally laid down they are soft; they become compacted by the weight of overlying sediments to produce shales, sandstones and conglomerates.

Metamorphic rocks result from the alteration of igneous and sedimentary rocks by the pressure and heat which accompanies the great bending and breaking movements in the earth's crust which produce great mountain ranges. This crustal folding and fracturing has been a common occurrence throughout the history of our planet and has often been accompanied by the movement of large masses of magma in the surface layers of the crust. The high pressures, high temperatures and the chemical activity associated with these events cause sedimentary and igneous rocks to be so greatly changed in appearance and composition that they are renamed metamorphic rocks (e.g. gneiss, schist, marble).

Perhaps the way in which these various rock types are related may best be understood with reference to a simple model (*Fig. 5*). If we assume an initial continental land area consisting of igneous rock and bounded by an ocean, the land area is subject to attack by geomorphological processes. Igneous material is eroded and transported by rivers out into the ocean basin where the eroded rock fragments accumulate in layers to form sedimentary rock. Subsequently, earth movements fold these sediments to create a new mountain system and the sedimentary rocks are uplifted and folded to produce a new land area. At the time of folding new molten magma is forced up through the old igneous rocks and into the new sedimentary rocks. The pressures of folding and the heat released during the intrusion of the new igneous material causes both the old igneous rocks and some of the new sedimentary rocks to be changed into metamorphic rocks. The new land surface, formed by all three types of rock, is then subjected to the processes of erosion to produce distinctive landforms. These same processes contribute more sediment for accumulation in the ocean basin. This sequence of events may take many millions of years.

Although the evolution of the planet earth within the solar system goes back over 4,500 million years, the oldest rocks in Scotland – the metamorphic rocks in the Outer Hebrides – are approximately 2,600 million years old. In Scotland, therefore, we have little evidence of the evolution of the earth's crust during the first 2,000 million years of its existence. The ancient metamorphic rocks (mainly gneiss) must have suffered severe erosion and supplied sediment to an adjacent sea. These sediments became transformed into what we now call the Torridonian Sandstones which outcrop at the surface along a belt stretching from Cape Wrath to Skye. The sand forming these sandstones was deposited in shallow seas and was derived from a land surface to the north-west which was experiencing a desert climate. Only micro

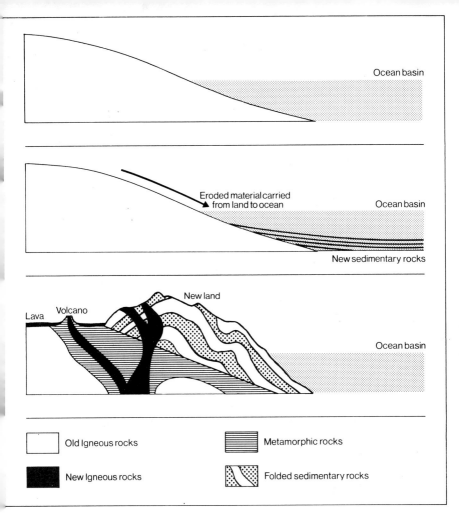

Old Igneous rocks

Metamorphic rocks

New Igneous rocks

Folded sedimentary rocks

5. A simplified model of the geological evolution of part of the earth's crust. This sequence of events could take hundreds of millions of years to be completed.

fossils of plankton have been found in these rocks, all of which belong to what is known as the Pre-Cambrian Era. It was not until the succeeding Cambrian Era (600–500 million years ago) that the first macro fossils, representing early life forms (shell fish and crustacea) occur.

The sort of time periods so far discussed are of a range which is very difficult to comprehend. Hundreds and thousands of millions of years mean very little in the human time scale. Comprehension is made easier if we equate the age of the earth (4,500 million years) to one 24 hour period. It is then possible to place the more

important events in geological history into perspective and particularly to notice how little we know about most of the earth's history.

Although our knowledge of the early phases of the geological
history of Scotland is very sketchy, these early phases had a very
important effect on the distribution of the rock types we now see at
the surface in the Highlands and Islands. By about 400 million years
ago (on our 24 hour scale, 10.00 p.m.) most of the rocks that now
make up this region, and in particular the major geological
structures which give so many of the landforms their familiar
north-east to south-west alignment, had been established.

About 350 million years ago sediments derived from the uplifted
Caledonian mountains were deposited in shallow seas. These
sediments were also eventually uplifted to produce the extensive
sandstone lowlands of the Moray Firth area, Caithness and
Orkney. Between 70 and 50 million years ago (11.40 p.m. on the 24
hour scale) there was a very important outburst of volcanic activity
which affected the Inner Hebrides, parts of Argyll and Arran.
Massive volcanoes and extensive lava flows buried the older rocks.
This activity was accompanied by faulting and uplift. Unfortunately, there is virtually no record of the geological events which took
place in the Highlands and Islands between the end of the Tertiary
volcanic activity and the beginning of the Ice Age about 3 million
years ago (11.59 p.m. on the 24 hour scale). There are no rocks
younger than the Tertiary volcanics within the region and much of
the record of erosion and landform development of the period was
destroyed by glacial processes during the Ice Age. We will probably
be able to learn a great deal about what happened on the land area
over the last 50 million years from the information that is now being
made available from the exploration of the sediments in the
offshore zone by oil companies. The sediments should reveal the
history of erosion on the adjacent land area.

The last major event in the geological history of the Highlands
and Islands was the repeated invasion of the area by glaciers and ice
sheets during the last 3 million years. The imprint of these events is
relatively clear compared with the earlier periods of geological
history that they will be discussed in detail in a later section. After
the retreat of the last glaciers about 10,000 years ago it was not long
before man came on the scene. The earliest records of man's
occupation of the region suggest that he arrived about 8,000 years
ago – about two-tenths of a second before midnight on the 24 hour
scale.

The magnitude of the geological events which created the main rock types and structures of the Highlands and Islands is difficult to appreciate. The creation of land areas is primarily the result of earth movements generated by energy derived from the interior of the earth. Uplift, folding and faulting create land areas which are then progressively eroded away by the work of running water, moving ice, wind or waves. We can only observe the results of major earth movements because the only movements of the crust which are going on at present are on a very much smaller scale or are proceeding at such a slow rate that they are not comparable with the great mountain building episodes of the past. However, the main processes of erosion, transportation and deposition at work on the earth's surface today are assumed to be similar to those that have attacked the continental areas throughout geological time. The rate at which these processes proceed is very slow. Throughout the Scottish Highlands, erosion is proceeding at a rate which produces a loss of rock debris of between 10 and 50 tonnes per square kilometre per year. This is likely to produce a lowering of the land surface of between 1 and 5 cm per thousand years. When these rates of erosion are extended over the tens of millions of years of geological time, it is not surprising that great mountain chains similar to the Rocky Mountains or the Himalayas could be reduced to lowlands by these seemingly slow processes.

The history of the earth's surface is dominated by the endless battle between uplifted parts of the earth's crust and the erosional attack of the geomorphological machine. The rocks and the landforms of any area provide information about the geological events and the landforming processes which have occurred in the past. Any attempt to determine the geological history and the origin of the landforms of an area is dependent on the existence of evidence in the form of materials and shapes which can be interpreted. Clearly, if rocks and landforms of one period are destroyed by events in a subsequent period, then there will be large gaps in the story. This is the case for the Highlands and Islands where, although very ancient and very young rocks and forms are present, many of the intermediate events have been obliterated.

Rock Type and Structures

The dominant rock type found in the Highlands and Islands is metamorphic (*Fig. 6*). Large areas consist of rocks which are very

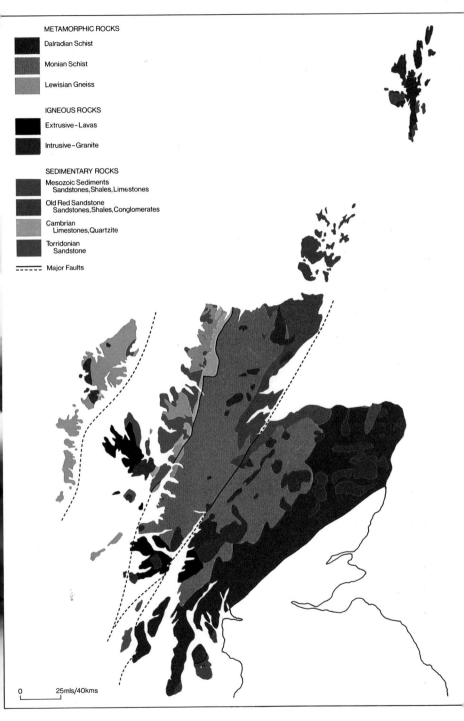

METAMORPHIC ROCKS

Dalradian Schist

Monian Schist

Lewisian Gneiss

IGNEOUS ROCKS

Extrusive-Lavas

Intrusive-Granite

SEDIMENTARY ROCKS

Mesozoic Sediments
Sandstones, Shales, Limestones

Old Red Sandstone
Sandstones, Shales, Conglomerates

Cambrian
Limestones, Quartzite

Torridonian
Sandstone

Major Faults

0   25mls/40kms

6. The distribution of solid rocks and major structures.

old and which have been altered by great pressures associated with mountain building episodes. The metamorphic rocks now on the surface are the roots of ancient mountain systems which have been largely eroded by later events.

In the north-west mainland and in the Outer Hebrides, Lewisian gneiss forms large areas. This rock type probably underlies the younger rocks of much of the rest of the Highlands. The gneiss was formed from greatly altered igneous and sedimentary rocks, the metamorphism having taken place between 2,600 million and 1,600 million years ago. Gneiss is a hard rock consisting of quartz, feldspar, mica and hornblende; it often shows a distinctive banding. This ancient rock takes on a variety of forms. In northern Lewis it underlies gently undulating areas while in southern Lewis and western Sutherland it forms mountains.

The large area of metamorphic rock on the mainland is subdivided into two groups on the basis of their age and structural history. The older of these two groups is known as the Moines and consists largely of schists and granulites. These rocks attain a maximum thickness of about 20,000 feet (6,000 m) with a conglomerate at the base which rests unconformably on the Lewisian gneiss. The relative uniformity of the Moine schists over great vertical thicknesses suggests that they represent the metamorphism of sediments deposited in the shallow water of a slowly subsiding basin. Some authorities believe that the Moinian rocks represent the metamorphism of rocks equivalent to the Torridonian sandstone.

The second and younger group of metamorphic rocks occupies the south-east Highlands in a zone from Kintyre to Buchan. They are known as the Dalradian and consist primarily of schists, grits, quartzite, and limestone. Because there is considerable vertical variation in this system, it is believed that they represent the metamorphism of sediments accumulating in a relatively rapidly subsiding basin in late pre-Cambrian and early Cambrian times. The Dalradian rocks are the main constituents of the Grampians and tend to produce smooth slopes and rounded summits in areas of high relative relief.

Both the Moinian and Dalradian rocks experienced great upheavals in what is known as the Caledonian mountain building episode which ended about 400 million years ago. At that time great mountain chains at least the size of the present day European Alps – and possibly similar in size to the Himalayas – were created by folding and faulting of the earth's crust. It was at this time that the basic grain of the Highlands was established. A great many structures were aligned in a north-east to south-west direction e.g. the Great Glen fault and the Highland Boundary fault (*Figs. 6 and 7*). Throughout the period of erosion that followed, these aligned structures influenced the development of subsequent geological events. The faulting continued over many millions of years and resulted in lateral displacement of anything from 5 miles (8 km) to 70 miles (112 km).

From the rock type map (*Fig. 6*) it can be seen that there are numerous outcrops of granite (an intrusive igneous rock) throughout the Highlands and Islands. Granite is most common in the Grampians but significant outcrops also occur in Arran, Mull, Skye, Harris, Lewis and Sutherland. In most cases the granite forms rugged mountains as in Arran and Skye but in the Cairngorms the granite forms smooth plateau surfaces. On Rannoch Moor the granite is associated with the floor of a basin surrounded by mountains. The granites were intruded at various times: most of those in the Grampians were intruded between 400 and 350 million years ago while those of Arran, Mull and Skye were intruded 60

7.   The Great Glen. A fault controlled valley.

million years ago. Associated with the more recent granite intrusions on Mull and Skye are volcanic rocks which solidified on the earth's surface (extrusive igneous activity). These rocks are known as basalt and have a distinctive stepped appearance created by the subsequent erosion of individual lava flows.

Sedimentary rocks only occupy a relatively small percentage of the area of the Highlands and Islands. Apart from small outcrops in such localities as Mull, Morven, and Arran there are two main areas covered by consolidated sediments : a coastal zone 10 to 20 miles (16 to 32 km) wide stretching from Cape Wrath to the Sound of Sleat, and an east coast area extending from around the shores of the Moray Firth through Caithness to Orkney. These two areas of sedimentary rock are very different. The western area consists of Pre-Cambrian and Cambrian sandstone and limestone, which are 800 to 500 million years old, whereas the eastern area consists of Devonian sandstone and shales 400 to 350 million years old.

The great contrast in the north-west Highlands between the basement of Lewisian gneiss and the overlying Torridonian sandstone is quite remarkable. The Torridonian sandstone is the oldest sedimentary rock within the region. It consists of sandstones, grits and pebble beds which have been very little metamorphosed, attaining a maximum total thickness of over 1,600 feet (480 m). The main characteristic of these sediments is their well-bedded structure which produces a distinctive step like morphology to their surface form. These sediments were derived from the erosion of Lewisian gneiss on a land area experiencing desert conditions, the products of erosion being redeposited in shallow seas. After deposition, earth movements uplifted these sediments and they too were exposed to erosion so that large areas of Torridonian sandstone were completely removed to reveal the underlying Lewisian gneiss. In the Outer Hebrides only a small area of Torridonian rock survives near Stornoway; in the Inner Hebrides there are important outcrops of Torridonian on Skye, Rhum, Colonsay and Islay. However, it is the distinctive pyramidal mountains of Ross and Sutherland (e.g. Suilven, Quinag and the massive, stepped mountains of the Torridon district) which are the best expressions of these sediments.

Somewhat younger than the Torridonian sediments, and occurring in a narrow outcrop from Durness to the Sound of Sleat, are the Cambrian sediments. They are mainly limestones and quartzites (metamorphosed sandstone).

Both Torridonian and Cambrian sediments only occur to the west of one of the most distinctive structures in Scotland – the Moine Thrust. This structure consists of a series of low angle fault planes along which great masses of rock have been moved many miles. The Moine schists were carried north-westwards over the Cambrian, Torridonian and Lewisian formations. A major feature resulting from this zone of thrusts is westward facing escarpments that have been produced as a result of erosion of the rocks above the thrust planes.

Whereas the western area of sedimentary rocks is characterised by great mountain and valley systems, the eastern area – occupied by Devonian sediments – is characterised either by lowlands, e.g. around the shores of the Moray Firth, Caithness and most of the Orkney Islands, or by smooth rounded hills (e.g. the northern part of the island of Hoy). It is highly likely that these Devonian sediments extended much further west, particularly in Sutherland, and have been removed by erosion to reveal the older Moine schists.

There are only very small pockets of sedimentary rocks younger than those of Devonian age in the Highlands and Islands. Rocks of Triassic, Jurassic and Cretaceous age occur in small outcrops on Skye, Mull, Arran and around the shores of the Moray Firth but they are insignificant in terms of the landforms developed throughout the region as a whole.

There remain two groups of sediments, neither of which are shown on figure six, to which I must refer. Resting on top of the metamorphic, igneous and sedimentary rocks is a widespread but relatively thin cover of unconsolidated sediments. These sediments were laid down during the Pleistocene period commonly referred to as the Ice Age.

About three million years ago a deterioration in climate led to the build up of glaciers and ice sheets resulting in major changes in sea level around the Scottish coasts. The glaciers expanded and retreated several times, each succeeding period of glaciation largely destroying the deposits of the previous glaciation. This means that it is only the deposits of the last glaciation – which began about 27,000 years ago – and its associated changes in sea level that have survived.

Large areas of the Highlands and Islands are covered by glacial deposits which range in thickness from one foot (0.3 m) to 100 feet (30 m). Deposits laid down by the ice itself, consisting of a wide

8.   Glacial till – angular fragments of various sizes embedded in silt and clay.

9.   Fluvioglacial sands and gravels laid down by water produced by melting glaciers. The rock fragments are rounded and arranged in layers.

variety of generally angular or sub-angular rock fragments embedded in a matrix of fine material, usually silt or clay, are known as till (*Fig. 8*). They occur extensively in thin sheets over the lower slopes throughout the region. Deposits produced by the meltwaters associated with the glaciers consist of sands and gravels laid down by rivers flowing off the ice (*Fig. 9*). These sands and gravels originally covered the floors of many valleys within the Highlands to depths of between 10 and 200 feet (3 to 60 m) but much of this material has been eroded away during the last ten thousand years.

One further group of deposits remains. I have mentioned already that, as the glaciers expanded and retreated, sea level fluctuated. Evidence of these fluctuations occurs in the form of beach materials –mainly sand and gravel – left stranded up to 130 feet (39 m) above present sea level. These deposits are best preserved around the Inner Hebrides, in Argyll and around the Moray Firth.

Figure 6 and the above comments give a general outline of the geology of the Highlands and Islands of Scotland. It is very obvious that the rocks that make up this region vary widely in age and type and that it is not possible to explain the distribution of high ground and low ground purely in terms of geological variations. Some of the oldest and hardest rocks in Scotland form lowlands in Lewis while some of the youngest consolidated rocks, the Tertiary volcanic igneous rocks, form very high ground in Skye and Mull. Now we must see what evidence there is for the evolution of the landforms themselves. It is inevitable that the most recent events in the geological history of an area are most likely to be the most important in terms of landform evolution. In Scotland by far the most significant recent geological event has been the covering of the land by glaciers and ice sheets. Glaciation is so important to an understanding of the landforms of the Highlands and Islands that a separate section will be devoted to it. Firstly, we must determine what the region was like before the glacial period.

PREGLACIAL LANDFORMS

In order to determine the evolution of the landforms of an area there must either be deposits present – which indicate the nature of the erosion and deposition which have taken place – or relics of the landforms themselves. Over most of the Highlands and Islands, the solid rocks are either several hundred million years old or even thousands of millions of years old. Were these ancient rocks once covered by much younger rocks which were subsequently removed by erosion? Or, have they remained uncovered and subject to continued erosion ever since they were thrown up into great mountain chains in the Caledonian mountain building movements some 400 million years ago? Since most of the region neither has rocks nor distinctive forms which can be proved to be less than 400 million years old, except of course the Tertiary volcanic rocks of the Inner Hebrides and the glacial deposits, it has to be admitted that whatever is said about the evolution of the preglacial landforms is little more than informed guess work.

After the build up of the volcanic materials in the Inner Hebrides, in Morvern and on Arran there is a blank in the geological record. The worn down roots of the Caledonian mountains, the partially stripped cover of the Torridonian sandstone in the north-west, the ancient metamorphic rocks of Sutherland and the Outer Hebrides, the new volcanic forms of the Inner Hebrides and the sandstones of the north-east were then subjected to some 50 million years of erosion. We know that the period of erosion was very severe as only the roots of the Hebridean volcanoes have survived. It is probable that the climate over this 50 million year period was at least moist and temperate; probably at times it was sub-tropical. This would allow weathering of the surface rocks to progress rapidly; the weathered material would migrate down slope towards the stream channels which would act as drains moving this material to the adjacent seas.

The best of detectives cannot re-create a crime without any evidence. Geologists and geomorphologists simply do not have enough evidence to re-create the story of the geological and landform changes which affected the Highlands and Islands during this period. There are two lines of deduction which are worth mentioning. Firstly, the pattern created by the river systems – the drainage pattern – seems to cut across many of the rock types and structures of the region. Secondly, there appears to be a concordance of summit altitudes at various levels throughout the Highlands. This suggests that many of the mountains represent the erosional remnants of formerly extensive upland surfaces.

The development of river systems is controlled by three basic factors – the nature of the original surface on which they occur; the nature of the climate at the time of their development; and the location of the base-level (i.e. ocean basin) to which they are linked. If the river systems of the Highlands and Islands had developed on the surface produced by the Caledonian earth movements it would be dominated by major north-east to south-west oriented river systems. This relationship is exhibited by the Great Glen, the Spey Valley and the Upper Tay Valley, but there are a large number of valleys which are aligned north-west to south-east or west to east.

This occurrence of a discordant drainage pattern suggested to early authorities that perhaps the region had been completely covered by a layer of rocks upon which the drainage system was established; then, as these rivers cut down through this layer, they became superimposed on the older rocks beneath. With the exception of the Pleistocene deposits, rocks of Cretaceous age – on the floor of the North Sea and in small outcrops in Mull, in Morvern and on Eigg, Skye and Raasay – are the youngest sedimentary rocks which could have covered the region. It seems likely that these scattered outcrops of Cretaceous rock represent a once more widespread occurrence of Cretaceous material. But there is no evidence that the Highlands were once buried beneath a Cretaceous cover on which the drainage system developed.

There is no doubt, however, that after the deposition of Cretaceous material, there was up-lift and widespread erosion. On this eroded surface, developed in early Tertiary times (70 million years ago), the volcanoes and basalts of Skye and Mull were laid down. These lava piles reached thicknesses of the order of 6,000 feet (1,800 m) but were restricted in their distribution: there is no evidence of them ever having occurred in the Outer Hebrides or on the mainland beyond Morvern. The fact that dykes (intrusive sheets of igneous material) of Tertiary age were truncated by subsequent erosion and that valleys have been cut through these dykes indicates that the drainage system and the surface upon which it developed are both younger than the Tertiary volcanic period. It seems likely, therefore, that the Highlands were up-lifted some 30 million years ago in the form of a gently sloping eroded surface with a general slope towards the south-east. In what is believed to be a sub-tropical climate, a drainage system developed with the longest rivers flowing towards the east and south-east with a watershed within 20 miles (32 km) of the west coast. The detailed evolution of the landforms on this uplifted block is very difficult to interpret. Some believe that a series of erosion surfaces related to changing sea levels can be interpreted from the concordance of summit altitudes in various parts of the Highlands. Since these surfaces were created prior to the glacial period, they will have suffered severe frost shattering and glacial erosion. It seems very unlikely that much of the true preglacial surface still remains.

We know very little about the details of the forms created in preglacial times. The major areas of high ground and low ground had been established along with the valley network before glaciation started. The large part of the Highlands and Islands underlain by metamorphic rocks and their associated igneous intrusions was a dissected upland with considerable areas above 2,500 feet (750 m) in altitude. The area of complex lithology and structure west of the Moine Thrust and the areas of Tertiary volcanic activity were mountainous in character, albeit less rugged than they eventually became after glaciation.

The only areas of extensive lowland within the region were the areas of Old Red Sandstone rocks around the Moray Firth and on the Orkneys and areas of Lewisian gneiss in western Sutherland and the Outer Hebrides. In other words, the basic framework of landform distribution had been established during the Tertiary Period (70 million to 3 million years ago) but, because of the intensity of erosion during the Pleistocene Ice Age, it is impossible to determine the details of landform evolution during this critical period.

THE EFFECTS OF GLACIATION

The idea that large parts of the earth's surface were once covered by glaciers and ice sheets has only received wide acceptance during the last 130 years. The glacial theory was introduced to Scotland by a Swiss scientist, Louis Agassiz, in 1840. It was quickly taken up by Scottish geologists so that Scotland became a leading area for research into the effects of glaciation in the latter half of the nineteenth century.

The previous greater extent of glaciers and ice sheets was deduced by analogy. Similar deposits and landforms to those which occur near existing glaciers in Switzerland, Norway, Greenland and Iceland were observed in Scotland and it was therefore agreed that glaciers once existed in Scotland. These forms and deposits were the latest products of geological processes; therefore, glaciation must have occurred relatively recently in geological time. The actual dating of the glacial events has only been possible with the development of radiometric dating techniques such as carbon[14] or potassium/argon methods. It has been established that approximately 3 million years ago there was a gradual cooling of the atmosphere in middle and high latitudes; there began a period of fluctuating cold and mild climates which is still with us. During the cold intervals, areas which previously had received most of their precipitation in the form of rain changed to the situation in which most of the precipitation arrived as snow. Once sufficient snow fell to allow snow patches to last from one winter to the next, these snow patches began to expand and the snow became transformed into glacier ice. The advent of a glacial period interrupted the normal fluvial cycle, in which water is evaporated from the ocean, carried over the land masses by winds to be released in the form of rain to return to the oceans via the rivers. Once snow and ice began to accumulate on the land surface, the only way that water could be returned to the oceans was for the ice to flow down the valleys as glaciers to reach lower altitudes where melting could take place. Because this cold climate cycle was slower than the normal fluvial cycle, large masses of water were trapped in the ice sheets; the water volume in the oceans fell so that there was a general lowering of sea level by 300 feet (100 m) during periods of glaciation.

The areas most suitable for the accumulation of snow and ice during a period of glaciation are those which receive large amounts of precipitation and which have high local relief values at middle or high latitudes. Most of the Scottish Highlands (Lat 56-58°N) have these characteristics. It is not surprising that they developed glaciers once the cooling period was initiated.

The most recent events in geological time are similar to all the earlier ones in that it is only from the deposits and forms they produced that the events themselves can be determined. Even in the relatively recent past the same principle applies; because glaciation only produces unconsolidated sediments, it is not surprising that, except in certain favoured localities, the deposits of early glaciations were destroyed by subsequent glaciations. From other parts of Europe and North America the ice sheets are known to have advanced and retreated several times – as many as ten times in some places. How many times the Scottish ice sheet built up and then retreated is not known accurately, although evidence from England suggests that this sequence occurred several times. Most of what we know about the glaciation of Scotland is based on the evidence relating to the last ice sheet which began to develop about 27,000 years ago and which finally wasted away about 17,000 years later. It is generally assumed that the earlier ice sheets behaved in a similar manner.

A period of glaciation is started when the snow line (i.e. the level at which the snow remains from one winter to the next) is progressively lowered. The best areas for snow accumulation have high relative relief values and high precipitation. Within the Highlands and Islands, the main area of ice accumulation coincided with the zone of high ground stretching from Cape Wrath to the Firth of Clyde. These west facing slopes received large amounts of precipitation; when a considerable portion began to fall as snow, permanent snow banks started to form on the high ground and in the valley heads (*Fig. 12*). With continued deterioration of climate, the snow banks thickened and the snow was converted to glacier ice. During the early phases of glaciation the glaciers were confined by the pre-existing valleys (*Fig. 10*); eventually they became so

10. During the early stages of glaciation the glaciers are confined by valley sides.

11. At the full extent of glaciation most of the land is covered by ice.

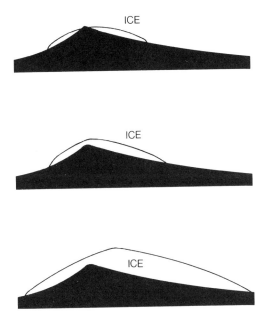

12.   Valley glaciers build up into an ice cap and then into an ice-sheet.

thick that even the intervening ridges became buried and an ice cap developed (*Fig. 11*). Its greatest altitude roughly coincided with the former watershed between the short streams flowing to the west coast and the longer streams flowing to the east coast (*Fig. 12*). This new ice surface became the site for new accumulation. Then all the ice cap became thicker and, eventually, the ice divide was displaced eastward of the former watershed.

While the main ice cap was developing in the western mountains of the mainland (*Fig. 13*) other local centres of ice accumulation developed on the islands of Skye, Rhum, Mull and Arran in the west and in the Cairngorms and Monadhliath Mountains in the east. The ice moved outwards from these centres, the lines of movement being recorded by fragments of rock which occur in the glacial deposits known as erratics (a piece of rock which does not occur locally but has been transported from another area by glacier ice). Distinctive rock outcrops – such as the Rannoch, Etive and Glen Fyne granites – can be traced as the sources from which rock fragments in the glacial deposits of the surrounding areas were derived. Their existence permits maps of the lines of ice movement to be compiled (*Fig. 14*).

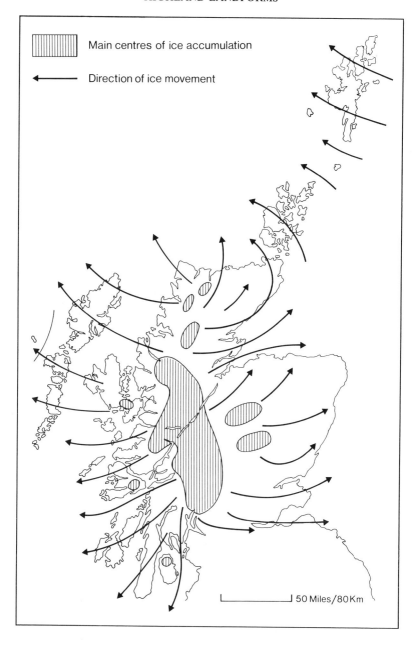

13.   The main centres of ice accumulation were in the Western Highlands.

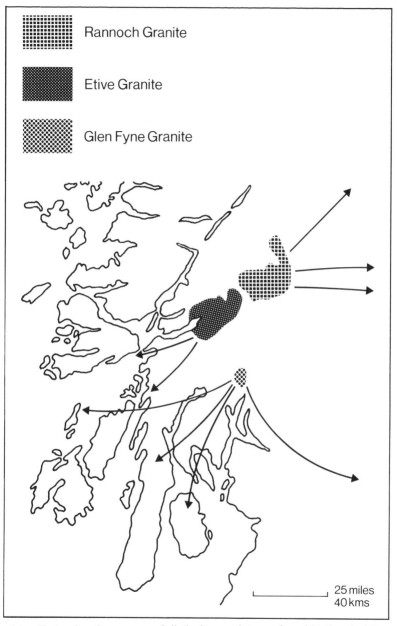

14. By tracing the sources of distincitve rock types found in the glacial deposits, the direction of movement of the glaciers, which laid down the deposits, can be determined.

The various centres of ice accumulation eventually coalesced to produce an ice sheet which completely buried all the Highlands and Islands. It is unlikely that even the highest peaks stood above the surface of the ice since it is possible that the highest parts of the ice surface attained a maximum altitude of between 4,000 feet (1,200 m) and 5,000 feet (1,500 m). Individual ice streams within the ice sheet attained thicknesses of 1,000 feet (300 m) to 3,000 feet (900 m) and they probably moved at rates of between 30 feet (9 m) and 600 feet (180 m) per year.

The outer limits of the last ice sheet are not well known. To the west, ice from the mainland crossed the Minch and continued westward across the Outer Hebrides beyond the Flannan Isles and North Rona but not as far as St. Kilda. In the east, Scottish ice moved out onto the floor of the North Sea but was probably not in contact with ice from Scandinavia. The Grampians were a major source for ice that moved south into the Central Valley of Scotland where it met ice originating in the Southern Uplands. Since the major source of the Highland ice was in the south-west Grampians, one stream of Highland ice continued south down the Firth of Clyde and carried Highland rocks to the Isle of Man and to the coast around the southern Irish Sea. A second stream of Highland ice turned eastwards past the site of Glasgow towards the site of Edinburgh and continued southwards along the east coast of Scotland.

The build up of the last Scottish ice sheet coincided with ice accumulation on the high ground in Northern England, Ireland and Wales, so that by 18,000 years ago the whole of Britain north of the sites of Hull, Birmingham, Cardiff and Dublin was covered by ice. A mere 5,000 years later virtually all of this ice had disappeared and, apart from a re-advance of ice between 11,000 and 10,000 years ago which only affected the original centres of accumulation in the high ground of Scotland, the last major environmental change in Britain had come to an end. We must now examine what this and other periods of glaciation did to modify the landforms which existed prior to glaciation.

The main effect of the change in the normal hydrological cycle which results in glaciation is that instead of precipitation returning to the ocean basins by relatively fast moving water flowing in confined channels on valley floors, the precipitation returns to the oceans by means of slow moving glaciers which occupy all the cross section of the valleys. Glacier ice itself is not very hard and is not

15. A corrie, Ben Lawers.

16. A glacial-trough, Loch Avon, Cairngorms.

capable of very much erosion. Nearly all glaciers, however, pick up rock fragments in their lower layers so that the underside of a glacier is rather like a piece of sand paper. As the glaciers move forward under the force of gravity they erode the rock surfaces over which they pass.

The main modifications to pre-existing valleys produced by glacial erosion are the over-deepening of valley heads to produce armchair hollows known as cirques or corries (*Fig. 15*). After several periods of glaciation, quite massive mountains are progressively eaten away by corrie development to leave a series of jagged peaks and ridges. As ice moves through valley systems, the sides of the valleys tend to be straightened and steepened and the floors deepened. A typical glaciated valley is trough like with straight steep, sides (*Fig. 16*). The floors of these valleys are often over-deepened with basins gouged out of their floors by glacial erosion. Some of these ice gouged basins attain considerable depths, e.g. Loch Morar 1,017 feet (305 m), Loch Ness 754 feet (226 m), Loch Lomond 623 feet (187 m), Loch Ericht 512 feet (153 m). Many of the glacial troughs and basins within the Highlands coincide with fault lines where earth movements have provided zones of crushed rock which both the preglacial rivers and the glaciers found relatively easy to erode.

Undoubtedly, evidence of glacial erosion is most dramatic in mountain areas where the corries and troughs form the major elements in the scenery. Glacial erosion also occurs on lowlands and plateaus. On the isle of Lewis and in Sutherland large areas of gneiss have been moulded into monotonous landscapes consisting of small hills and hollows. This type of country is often referred to as 'knob and lochan' (*Fig. 17*). Each of the knobs is usually smoothed on the side facing the advancing ice and is rather jagged on the downstream side where the moving ice has plucked away blocks of rock. The hollows between the rock knobs are produced by glacial erosion and are either filled with peat or small lochs.

The erosional activity of ice was not limited to what is now the land area of the Highlands and Islands. During the height of the glacial period, when so much water was locked up in the ice sheet, sea level dropped by three hundred feet (100 m) and the glaciers gouged deep channels between Skye and the mainland, Rhum and Skye, Mull and the mainland, Loch Linnhe, the Sound of Jura and on either side of Arran. Most of these off-shore troughs are between 400 feet (120 m) and 800 feet (241 m) deep and their

17. Knob and lochan terrain.

formation during the Ice Age resulted in the creation of numerous islands which, in preglacial times, were a part of the mainland.

The ability of glaciers to erode is matched by their ability to transport the eroded material and re-deposit it. Material is transported on their surface and within the ice. When the ice melts, the material in transport is released to form a characteristically unsorted, unstratified material called till (*Fig. 8*). The material carried in the basal layers of the ice melts out to produce a compact deposit resting on the bedrock. These till sheets are very extensive in the Highlands and Islands and are a very important surface material on the lower slopes of even the highest and most rugged areas. They are also important as parent materials for soils. The till cover often gives a more gentle appearance to areas within the region simply because the till occupies the erosional hollows in the bedrock. As well as occurring in sheets, till can also form distinctive ridges and mounds known as moraines. Along the lateral and frontal margins of glaciers, debris can accumulate, by melting and slumping, in the form of a ridge which marks the location of a halt in the general retreat of the glacier. In other circumstances the amount of debris accumulation is so great that the glacier ice becomes completely buried with boulders, gravel, sand and clay.

18. Morainic mounds, Glen Torridon.

Eventually the ice beneath this debris melts out and a series of hills 10 feet (3 m) to 50 feet (15 m) high are produced (*Fig. 18*). These morainic mounds give a wild aspect to the floor of many a Highland glen.

Really good examples of moraine ridges and mounds are limited to those parts of the Highlands and Islands where ice lasted longest. Most of Scotland was ice free by about 13,000 years ago but a return to cold conditions brought about an advance of the glaciers between 2,000 and 3,000 years later. Because this advance was first recognised along the southern shores of Loch Lomond it is known as the Loch Lomond Advance. During that thousand year period glaciers re- occupied the valleys of the high ground on the west side of the mainland and descended down to sea level on the west coast. Small ice caps developed on the mountains of Harris and Lewis, Skye, Rhum, Mull and Arran as well as on the Cairngorms and Monadhliath Mountains. The extent of this advance can usually be clearly seen in the freshness of the morainic features in the valleys occupied by the last glaciers to occur in Scotland.

When the glaciers of the Highlands and Islands began to melt, vast quantities of water were released and flowed on, in and under the glaciers themselves and down the valleys as they became ice free. The lower ends of some valleys remained blocked by ice while the upper ends were ice free. This allowed large and deep lakes to develop with glacier ice acting as the dam. The most famous example of such ice dammed lakes within the Highlands was in Glen Roy where the lake lasted sufficiently long for shorelines to develop along the valley side. In many cases, meltwater flowed between the glacier and the valley side, the streams cutting channels in locations where no normal river would flow (*Fig. 19*).

The obvious routes for most of the meltwaters to follow during the retreat of the glaciers were the preglacial valley floors. The rivers we now see in the Highland glens were increased in volume many times during the summer melt periods. The retreating glaciers which were feeding these rivers were also heavily laden with boulders, gravel and sand. This material was deposited on the valley floors creating the broad flat floors consisting largely of stratified gravel and sand (*Fig. 9*) which occur throughout the Highlands. After all the glacially derived material was deposited by these rivers the rivers began to cut into their own deposits to produce the many fine river terraces (*Fig. 20*) which now occupy these valleys.

Some of the meltwater streams deposited sand and gravel under the ice in tunnels. These deposits form very distinctive ridges 10 feet (3 m) to 50 feet (15 m) in height, often sinuous in plan and with tributary ridges joining the main ridge. The ridges are known as eskers. Other meltwater streams deposited sand and gravel on top of lumps of melting glacier ice. When the buried ice eventually melted away, enclosed depressions were created in the deposits producing a series of hollows separated by mounds. This hummocky form, known as kame and kettle topography, is very similar to the morainic mounds produced by glacial deposition, the main difference being that kames (the mounds) consist of water-sorted sands and gravels.

It is not surprising that the vast amounts of meltwater released when the glaciers were retreating destroyed many of the landforms created by glacial deposition. The power of the meltwater rivers was enormous and most of the valley floor forms within the Highlands were created by them rather than by the glaciers.

As the Scottish ice sheet started to waste away, the highest peaks and ridges began to emerge above the ice surface. They did not find themselves in a pleasant mild environment but in a very harsh

19.   Meltwater channel cut by a stream produced by the melting of glacier ice.

20.   River Terraces, Glen Roy.

21. Screes.

environment which we now associate with high Alpine and Arctic locations. Although the glaciers had begun to waste away, at 3,000 feet (900 m) to 4,000 feet (1,200 m) the climate would have been very severe for several thousand years. This environment in which frost action would have been dominant is known as the periglacial environment. With the temperature frequently fluctuating around 0°C, water in cracks and crevices in the rock would alternatively freeze and thaw. The pressures produced when water expands on freezing in a confined space are enormous and are sufficient to break up even solid rock. The high altitude rock faces in the Highlands were exposed, therefore, to frost shattering. Great masses of rock debris moved down slope in the form of scree slopes (*Fig. 21*). Some of the more resistant pieces of solid rock were left upstanding on ridges and summits after the frost shattered material had moved down slope. These rock knobs are known as tors (*Fig. 22*). There are good examples on the summits of the Cairngorms.

The periglacial environment, which began as the first high ground became ice free, has continued up to the present day above 2,500 feet (750 m) in the Highlands and Islands. During the winter

22.   Tor produced by weathering of granite, Cairngorm.

the high altitude areas still experience very severe conditions; frost action is still at work producing screes and even creating patterns such as polygons and stone stripes on the summit areas. Since the disappearance of the last glacier about 10,000 years ago there have been minor changes of climate which have produced both milder and wetter conditions as well as periods of colder and more extensive periglacial environments than exist at present. These minor changes have not had a profound effect on the landforms and deposits produced by glaciation. It is perhaps worth remembering that it only requires a lowering of the mean summer temperature in some of the higher areas in the Highlands and Islands of Scotland by about 4° or 5°C for snow patches to survive from one winter to the next and for a period of glacier expansion to begin.

The build up of an ice sheet does not only produce important changes in landforms as a result of the erosional and depositional work of the ice and meltwater. The fact that a lot of water is held in the ice sheet produces a general lowering of sea level at the time of glacier expansion. This tendency is counteracted by the effect of the weight of ice on the land surface which causes a depression of the land and a relative rise in sea level. This rise and fall of the land is known as isostatic adjustment; the rise and fall of sea level due to changing amounts of water in the ocean basins is known as eustatic changes in sea level. The latter process is a part of world wide changes related to the build up and wastage of the great continental ice sheets, whereas isostatic changes are much more local in their effects.

There is no evidence of sea level changes around the Scottish coastline during the period of maximum ice cover, except perhaps the creation of glacial troughs in what is now the off-shore zone. As the glaciers began to retreat during the last glaciation, however, the land was still sufficiently depressed by the weight of the ice that, as the coastal area became ice free, sea level was relatively higher than it is at present. Since the ice lasted longest and reached its greatest thickness in the west central Highlands it is not surprising that the greatest isostatic depression and uplift occurred there. There is evidence of sea level changes in the form of uplifted shore platforms and beaches at altitudes up to 135 feet (40 m) between Ullapool and the Firth of Clyde on the west coast and up to 90 feet (27 m) around the shores of the Moray Firth. The north coast of Scotland, the Outer Hebrides and the Orkneys and Shetlands do not have raised marine features resulting from isostatic uplift.

There are excellent examples of raised rock platforms with sea
stacks and arches backed by beaches and abandoned cliffs com-
plete with caves (*Figs 23, 24*), which are clear testimony to the
higher sea levels which existed as the glaciers wasted away. Sands
and gravels transported by the meltwaters from the retreating
glaciers were brought down to the coast and built up into deltas
related to these higher sea levels (e.g. in Loch Linnhe at Corran
Ferry and Ballachulish and at the mouth of Loch Etive at Connel
Bridge.) The land continued to rise as the ice sheet wasted away
and the early coastal features began to be raised above sea level. It
was not long before the return of the water from the wastage of the
great continental ice sheets caused a eustatic rise in sea level.
About 8,000 years ago sea level began to rise faster than the land
was rising in Scotland and the deposits associated with this sea
(often referred to as the Neolithic or Flandrian Sea) are clearly seen
around the shores of mainland Scotland in the form of raised
beaches that reach altitudes of between 20 feet (6 m) and 40 feet (12
m) between Ullapool and the Firth of Clyde on the west coast and
20 feet (6 m) and 30 feet (9 m) around the shores of the Moray
Firth. The culmination in this post-glacial rise in sea level occurred
about 6,000 years ago. Since then sea level has been falling relative
to the land.

It can be clearly seen, therefore, that there have been some
major changes in the coastal configuration of the Highlands and
Islands, particularly of the west coast of the mainland and the Inner
Hebrides during the last 13,000 years. The generally indented
coastline of the Highlands and Islands suggests a certain amount of
drowning of the land. This perhaps is too great a simplification
because some of the great indentations result from erosion by
glaciers. At the same time there is evidence of fairly recent uplift
around most of the coast of the mainland. Only in Orkney,
Shetland and the Outer Hebrides is there convincing evidence of a
drowned coastline in the form of off-shore peat deposits. Around
the mainland coast uplift of varying amounts, since deglaciation
started, is known to have occurred. This uplift decreases in amount
in all directions outwards from a centre somewhere in the region of
Rannoch Moor. All the raised shorelines in Scotland are tilted.
Research has shown that they do not fall simply into the fourfold
classification of '100 feet', '50 feet', '25 feet' and '15 feet' so widely
referred to in the past.

Glaciation and its associated changes in sea level have made a

23.   Raised marine platform, cliff and arch, Port Appin, Argyll.

24.   Raised beaches, West Loch Tarbert, Jura.

great impact on the landforms of the Highlands and Islands. Although the basic framework was created by the interaction between the processes of fluvial erosion, transportation and deposition, and the various rock types and structures during the long period of the Tertiary (70 million years), it has been the events of the Pleistocene (the last 3 million years) – and in particular the various periods of glaciation – which have put the final touches to the form of the surface upon which man has had to live.

Landform Regions

The variety of scenery is one of Scotland's greatest natural assets but because it is so variable it is difficult to describe and explain. It is simply not possible in a book of this size to attempt a comprehensive description and explanation of the landforms of the Highlands and Islands. It is necessary, therefore, to divide the area into regions and to pick out one or two themes which can best be illustrated by each region. The complexity of the interaction between various processes and a wide range of rock types and structures over varying periods of geological time has provided a great variety of landforms. In trying to make generalisations about landforms, it is important to remember that the way in which you view a landform assemblage will influence your appreciation of the arrangement of the individual forms that make up the assemblage. For the majority of visitors the Highlands are viewed from the roadside and since most of the roads follow valley floors or coastal benches, the mountain wall dominates the view. For the hill walker and mountaineer, views from ridge crests or summits give a quite different perspective to the arrangement of landforms.

Although evidence of the work of glaciers dominates surface forms in the Highlands and Islands, variations in rock type and structure, geological history and preglacial landform characteristics allow the area to be subdivided into five regions. The mainland consists largely of two regions, one to the south and the other to the north of the Great Glen. Both of these regions are dominated by mountain and valley landforms. The extreme north-west of the mainland, plus the Outer Hebrides are characterised by very ancient rocks which either form undulating lowlands or massive but sometimes isolated mountains. The only really extensive lowlands in the area coincide with the occurrence of younger sedimentary rocks in Caithness, Orkney and around the Moray Firth. The islands of Skye, Rhum, Mull and Arran, along with the part of the mainland known as Ardnamurchan form the fifth region by virtue of the fact that they were all affected by Tertiary volcanic activity which is very much evident in the landforms.

THE GRAMPIANS

Two straight-line boundaries on the geological map (*Fig.* 6), the Great Glen fault and the Highland Boundary fault (which runs from Helensburgh in the south-west to Stonehaven in the north-east), encompass an area renowned for its mountain scenery. Although these mountains are not high compared with the Alps or the Himalayas, they have a very distinctive character. Only in Ben Nevis and the Cairngorms are there summits over 4,000 feet (1,200 m) but there are a great many other summits over 3,000 feet (900 m) within the region.

The Grampians are the worn down roots of a great mountain chain consisting of metamorphic rocks which were folded and faulted by the Caledonian earth movements which took place some 400 million years ago and which also created the Appalachian mountains in North America and the mountains of Norway and Sweden at the same time. The structures produced by these earth movements have a dominant alignment in a north-east to south-west direction as exemplified by the southern boundary fault of this region and the Great Glen fault. As a result of erosion along other fault lines and fold axes many of the coastal indentations (e.g. Loch Fyne, Loch Linnhe), fresh water lochs (Loch Awe, Loch Erricht, Loch Laggan and Loch Tay) and the main valley systems (Spey, Don, Dee, Tummel and Upper Tay) are also aligned from north-east to south-west. Even the shape of the Kintyre peninsula and the islands of Islay and Jura reflect the importance of these ancient structures.

Although the Grampians are dominated by metamorphic rocks (e.g. schist, slate, quartzite) there are also important occurrences of granite, particularly in the Cairngorms, on the Moor of Rannoch and in the Ben Nevis and Ben Cruachan areas. These various rock types and structures have experienced possibly hundreds of millions of years of attack by geomorphological agents. Erosion of

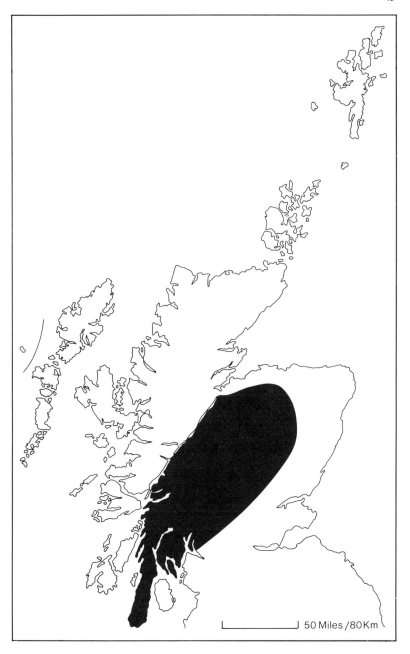

Map A.   The Grampians.

these ancient mountains provided sediment which accumulated in shallow seas in the North-east and in Central Scotland in Old Red Sandstone times (350 million years ago). They also suffered severe erosion under tropical conditions during the Carboniferous period (350–270 million years). How and when the major river valleys were developed is a matter of speculation but by the end of the Tertiary Period very little of the original Caledonian mountains was left. A series of north-easterly or easterly trending valleys originating in the Moor of Rannoch, plus a series of south-easterly trending valleys along the southern edge of the Highlands dominated the landform pattern. The watershed between rivers draining to the North Sea and those draining to the Atlantic was within 25 miles (40 km) of the west coast.

From the south, there are two main routes into the Grampian Mountains. In the east, Strath Tay and Glen Garry are followed by the A9 road from Perth to Inverness. Between Dunkeld and Pitlochry the valley floor is wide and there are massive river terraces cut out of the sand and gravels laid down by the meltwaters released as the last glaciers melted away. North of Pitlochry the valley narrows and in Glen Garry the traveller has his first experience of Highland landscape. Although absolute altitudes are not high (1,500–3,000 feet, 450–900 m), slopes are steep and strewn with boulders. Valley floors are often covered by innumerable mounds 10 to 30 feet (3 to 9 m) high which were formed from the debris carried by the last glaciers to invade the area. After crossing the summit of Drumochter Pass the A9 descends into the Spey Valley which has on either side two fine but very different mountain areas.

North-west of the Spey Valley are the Monadhliath Mountains or the grey mountains. They consist primarily of Dalradian schists and are characterised by a series of smooth ridges which attain heights of between 2,000 feet (600 m) and 3,000 feet (900 m). There is a general increase in altitude from north-east to south-west and a noticeable absence of corries and deep glacial troughs. The drainage pattern is closely related to the underlying Caledonian structures as is evidenced by the alignment of the Findhorn, Markie and Tarff rivers. What little evidence there is of the development of glacial corries is restricted to the south-east facing slopes which attain altitudes of 3,000 feet (900 m) above the Spey Valley. There is no doubt that this area was covered by the Scottish ice sheet during the last glaciation but it is unlikely that the Monadhliath

25. The Cairngorms, a granite massif.

Mountains themselves acted as a major accumulation area. Most of the ice to affect this area would have originated on the northern part of Rannoch Moor and in the mountains to the east and north-east of Ben Nevis.

South of the Spey Valley is one of the most impressive mountain areas in Scotland. The Cairngorm Mountains (*Figs 2 and 25*) consist of a series of peaks and ridges which attain altitudes of 3,500 feet (1,050 m) and 4,300 feet (1,290 m). These mountains consist of granite and they exhibit two contrasting landscapes. On the one hand there are smooth, rounded summit-areas broken only by upstanding rock knobs known as tors (*Fig. 22*) and on the other hand there are the deep troughs and corries which have so obviously been cut into the upper surface. In the west, Glen Einich cuts deeply into the massif with its rock walls some 2,000 feet (600 m) high. In the centre the massif is actually breached from north to south in two places. The most impressive breach is the Larig Ghru (*Fig. 26*) which cuts through the summit plateau between Ben Macdui and Braeriach as a narrow steep-sided valley nearly 1,000 feet (300 m) deep. The headwaters of the Derry Burn and a right bank tributary of the River Avon occupy the second breach. As

26. The Lairig Ghru: a glacial trough cut through the Cairngorms.

well as these breaches, the great glacial troughs of the Upper Dee and Avon along with some 40 individual corries bear witness to the severity of glacial erosion within the Cairngorms.

This granite massif constitutes the most extensive area over 3,000 feet (900 m) in Scotland. There has been a long debate about the origins of the upper surface of the Cairngorm plateau and the extent to which this plateau has been the source of the glacier ice which has so obviously cut the great troughs and corries. Some authors have suggested that the upper plateau surface has been little affected by ice and that it has remained largely in the form developed during the Tertiary period. Others believe that the upper plateau surface would have been an ideal accumulation zone for snow and ice during several glaciations and that it was glaciers descending from these plateau areas which cut the great troughs of the area. The majority view is that ice moving down the Spey and Dee valleys was joined by ice originating in the Cairngorms and it is hard to believe that any part of the Cairngorm massif remained ice free during the last glaciation.

The development of the Cairngorms as a major ski-ing resort is the result of the interaction of landforms and climate. Large areas of high ground result in significant amounts of precipitation falling as snow. Because of the detailed shape of the land, particularly the occurrence of high altitude corries, snow lies for long periods and allows ski-ing to continue well into the spring. The construction of chairlifts, which also operate in the summer, make the Cairngorm plateau accessible even to the most timid hill walker. A walk of a few miles from the top of the chairlift on Cairngorm allows close inspection of the frost shattered granite of the plateau surface and the core rocks left upstanding as tors. To the east can be seen the great glacial trough of Strath Nethy, to the south the rock basin of Loch Avon and cutting into the north-west face of the ridges a series of superb corries.

The Spey Valley itself is worthy of further comment. The source of the River Spey is in the mountains only a few miles east of the Great Glen and the river is remarkable, not only for its length and size of drainage basin, but also for its almost perfect alignment with the Caledonian structures. In preglacial times the cutting of the main Spey Valley and its many tributaries gave the main pattern of landforms in the eastern Grampians. With the onset of glaciation the areas of high ground and high precipitation in the headwaters of the Spey drainage basin formed a major centre of ice accumulation. Ice moved out from Rannoch Moor, via Glen Spean and the Ericht trough, to be joined by ice originating in the Monadhliath Mountains and the Cairngorms, to produce a glacier probably at least 2,000 feet (600 m) thick in the middle Spey Valley, and which moved out onto the coastal lowlands of the Moray Firth. When this enormous glacier melted away some 13,000 years ago, great quantities of water and debris were released which filled the floor of the Spey Valley with considerable thicknesses of sand and gravel. Over the last 10,000 years the River Spey has been eating into these deposits to produce its present flood plain and associated river terraces.

The second major routeway from the south into the Grampian Highlands is via Glasgow and Loch Lomond. The rapid transformation of the landforms as you cross the Highland Boundary Fault some five miles north of Balloch on the A82 is very impressive. The Loch Lomond basin narrows rapidly and descends to depths of over 600 feet (180 m) as it becomes surrounded by mountains which reach between 2,500 and 3,000 feet (750 and 900 m) (*Fig. 27*). The road north clings to the western shore of the rock basin and then climbs out of the northern end into the open but rugged floor of Glen Falloch.

27. Loch Lomond: the basin narrows northwards with Ben Lomond on
the right.

The journey north from Crianlarich to Fort William provides a
good cross section of the landforms of the south western Grampians. Deep but wide valleys surrounded by smooth hill slopes
rising to summit ridges about 3,000 feet (900 m) are typical of much
of the area developed on the Dalradian schists. Further to the
south-west, in mid-Argyll, similar forms extend down to the
indented coastline where the lower ends of glaciated valleys have
been invaded by the sea. For an area with mountains frequently
rising some 2,500 to 3,000 feet (750 to 900 m) above sea level there
are surprisingly few steep gradients on the roads that follow the
valley floors. The work of glacial erosion has been so severe that
many of the preglacial divides have been virtually completely
removed.

North of Loch Tulla on the A82 the landforms suddenly change.
Rannoch Moor is a bleak plateau area at an altitude of about 1,200
feet (360 m), surrounded by a rim of mountains between 2,500 feet
(750 m) and 3,500 feet (1,050 m). Much of Rannoch Moor is
underlain by granite which has experienced severe glacial erosion
to produce an irregular surface now characterised by numerous
small and irregularly shaped lakes separated by small rocky knolls
or hummocks of glacial debris. This plateau was the site of

accumulation for great masses of ice which moved out in all directions. This was where the last ice sheet to cover Scotland began to develop about 25,000 years ago and this is where it died away some 10,000 years ago. The radial patterns of the valleys leading from Rannoch Moor allowed ice to move to the north-east into the Spey basin, eastwards into the Tay system, southwards to the Firth of Clyde and westwards to Loch Linnhe, the Firth of Lorn and the Sound of Jura.

After crossing the Moor of Rannoch, the A82 suddenly plunges down into Glen Coe. The area between the Pass of Brander and Loch Lochy is one of the most spectacular in Scotland in terms of mountain landforms. It is interesting that by road, one descends into this area from the Rannoch plateau. This is because glacial erosion reduced the old preglacial drainage divide between the rivers leading to the Spey and Tay drainage systems and the shorter rivers leading to the Great Glen and Loch Linnhe. The A82 follows one of these low level cols to enter Glen Coe (*Fig. 28*) which is a deep glacial trough bounded by steep slopes rising to summit altitudes over 3,000 feet (900 m). The mountain landforms of this area appear to be more spectacular because they rise steeply from sea level.

28.   The entrance to Glen Coe from Rannoch Moor: a breached watershed.

The geological history of this part of the Grampians is rather complicated. Besides the metamorphic rocks which are so typical of much of the rest of the Grampians, there are important outcrops of granite, e.g. Ben Cruachan (3,689 feet, 1,107 m), Glenduror Forest (3,362 feet, 1,099 m) and Ben Nevis (4,406 feet, 1,322 m). Extrusive volcanic rocks also occur in Glencoe and on the summit of Ben Nevis.

In preglacial times a complicated drainage network must have been developed in this area and that valley system was further modified by intense glacial erosion. Every valley in this area has been deepened and straightened by glacial action and the intervening ridges frequently exhibit beautiful corries. The steep rock walls produced by glacial erosion makes this area very attractive to rock climbers. Some of the glacial troughs have been invaded by the sea to produce Loch Linnhe, Loch Etive, Loch Creran and Loch Leven (*Fig. 29*). A mere 10,000 years ago steep glaciers descended from the high ground into these troughs to discharge ice bergs which floated with the tide down Loch Linnhe and the Firth of Lorn.

29. Loch Leven: a glacial trough invaded by the sea. Ballachulish narrows at left – now bridged.

The granite mass of Ben Nevis with its capping of volcanic rock is Scotland's highest mountain (*Fig. 30*) (4,406 feet, 1,062 m). On a clear day the view from the summit gives the impression of wave after wave of land ridges stretching away in all directions. There is, however, one major break in the view and it is to the north. In that direction the Great Glen opens out as a major valley 1 to 3 miles (1.6 to 4.8 km) wide and over 50 miles (80 km) long (*Fig. 7*). It is continued below sea level in the Moray Firth to the north-east and in Loch Linnhe in the south-west. This remarkable feature coincides with the Great Glen fault, which is a major line of weakness in the earth's crust, that has resulted in relative movement of the rocks on either side of the fault of over 70 miles (110 km). The trend of the fault is parallel to the structures produced by the Caledonian earth movements and although the fault was initiated at the time of those earth movements, it has remained active throughout geological history. Even today, earth tremors are not uncommon along this fault line. In preglacial times, river systems tended to develop along the line of the fault and eroded the

30.   Ben Nevis viewed from the west. (Aero Films).

valley which runs from Fort William to Inverness. Glaciers occupied the valley, further eroding it to produce the rock basins of Loch Lochy and Loch Ness.

Before leaving the district of Lochaber I must mention the significance of this area in the development of ideas about the origin of Scottish landforms. In 1840 three men travelled by boat from Glasgow to Fort William. They were visiting the Highlands after a meeting of the British Association for the Advancement of Science in Glasgow where a Swiss scientist, Louis Agassiz, presented his ideas about a great ice sheet which had covered large parts of Europe in the recent geological past. Agassiz, accompanied by two famous British geologists, Buckland and Murchison, discovered, in the Lochaber district, deposits and landforms which clearly indicated to him that the area had been glaciated. In particular they visited Glen Roy where one of the most dramatic pieces of evidence relating to former glaciation can be seen. From the car park about four miles up Glen Roy, the sides of the upper glen can be seen to be marked by three horizontal lines (*Fig. 31*). The 'parallel roads' of Glen Roy and similar features in Glen Gloy and Glen Spean, have attracted more discussion than any other set

31.   Glen Roy: shorelines of former ice-amned lakes seen as parallel lines along hillside.

of landforms in Scotland. Traditionally they were believed to be hunting roads constructed by Fingal for the purpose of chasing deer but such an explanation was not acceptable in scientific circles. Agassiz, during his visit of 1840, suggested that they represented the shorelines of ice-dammed lakes, and this suggestion has since been convincingly demonstrated. During the late stages of the last glaciation ice moving eastwards from the areas of high precipitation to the west of the Great Glen entered Glen Spean where it was supplemented by ice from the Ben Nevis area and blocked off the southern ends of Glen Gloy and Glen Roy and the western end of Glen Spean (*Fig. 32*). Because they were dammed by ice, large lakes developed in each glen, the one in Glen Roy being 10 miles (16 km) long and 600 feet (180 m) deep. The maximum extent of each lake was determined by the altitude of the outlet cols at the head of each glen and the highest shoreline in each glen approximately occurs at the same altitude as the outlet col. The lower shorelines were formed as the lake levels fell.

Although the descriptions of the landforms along the two major routeways into the Grampian Highlands provide a general picture of the range of features to be seen there are certain exceptions

32. The probable position of the ice dam and the lakes which produced the 'parallel roads' of Glen Roy and Glen Gloy.

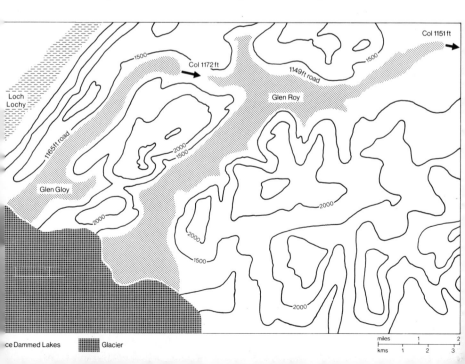

ce Dammed Lakes ▨ Glacier

miles 1 2

kms 1 2 3

which must be mentioned. For example, the area to the south-west of the Pass of Brander known as mid-Argyll, Knapdale, Kintyre and the islands of Jura and Islay are all a part of the Grampian mountains but the mountain ridges are not as high nor is the surface so rugged as the rest of the Grampians. The trend of the Caledonian structures is very strong but many of the ridges only reach altitudes of between 1,500 and 2,000 feet (450 and 600 m). Only in the area south of Oban are the Caledonian structures masked by a covering of Old Red Sandstone lavas which form the basis of a stepped land surface similar to that developed on the Tertiary lavas of Skye or Mull. Elsewhere, the repetition of north-east to south-west ridges often separated by lake basins or sea lochs provides a pleasant aspect particularly with the more widespread occurrence of trees on the lower slopes. A slight variation on this theme is to be found in the area between Loch Fyne and Loch Lomond where, although the ridge crests are somewhat higher, the alternation between land and water is both frequent and interesting. In the south-west Grampians, the preglacial valley system acted as an escape route for the Pleistocene glaciers most of which originated in the Rannoch Moor area. The Sound of Jura, Loch Fyne and the sea lochs leading to the Firth of Clyde have all been glacially modified.

Between Loch Lomond and Strath Tay the landforms are not so very different from those I have already described. There are a great many peaks over 3,000 feet (900 m) and several distinctive mountain masses. Most of the mountains consist of Dalradian schist but the conical mass of Schiehallion (3,547 feet, 1,064 m) consists of quartzite. Ben Lawers (3,984 feet, 1,195 m) is very typical of this area; the National Trust for Scotland Visitors Centre on the north side of Loch Tay provides interesting explanations in the form of models, maps, photographs and geological specimens of the geology and landforms of this area.

The Grampian Mountains are an excellent introduction to the landforms of the Highlands. They illustrate the importance of rock type and structure in the preglacial evolution of landforms and the drainage pattern. Although the whole area was inundated by ice during the Pleistocene the west suffered much more erosion than the east. The routes followed by the glaciers were largely determined by the alignment of the preglacial valleys but some preglacial watersheds were destroyed.

NORTH-CENTRAL HIGHLANDS

North of the Great Glen and extending for over 150 miles (240 km) from Morven in the south-west to the Sutherland coast in the north, is a belt of mountainous country between 30 and 40 miles (48 and 64 km) wide. Apart from a few areas of granite and an extension of the Mull Tertiary complex into Morvern and Ardnamurchan, this area is underlain by the Moine Series. These rocks have resulted from the metamorphism of sediments which are believed to be similar in age to the Torridonian sandstone. The main rock types are schists and granulites which were strongly folded in Ordovician and Silurian times.

The landforms of this region can be divided into three groups. South-west of Strath Bran is an area of mountains with summit altitudes between 3,000 and 3,800 feet (900 and 1,140 m). Between Strath Bran and Loch Shin there are extensive areas between 2,000 and 2,500 feet (600 and 750 m) with a few summits over 3,000 feet (900 m). North-east of Loch Shin several quite large but isolated mountains have summit altitudes between 2,500 and 3,000 feet (750 and 900 m) but they stand above an extensive undulating surface between 800 and 1,200 feet (250 and 360 m).

The present pattern of landforms in the North-central Highlands with the various groups of mountains separated by major valleys which either run from west to east or from north-west to south-east, is the result of the events which took place during the late Tertiary period. After extensive erosion the Moine rocks were uplifted in the form of a tableland with an eastward tilt and the drainage pattern which developed resulted in the dissection of this tableland. These original eastward flowing rivers produced the Helmsdale Valley, Loch Shin Valley, Strath Oykell and Strath Bran, Strath-farrar and Glen Shiel. The area to the south-west of Strath Bran, bounded on the north-west by the Sound of Sleat and on the south-east by the Great Glen and Loch Linnhe consists of a series

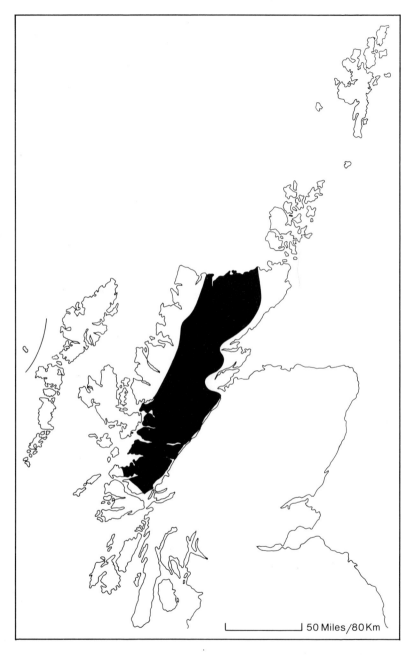

Map B.   North-Central Highlands

of ridges and valleys with a general west to east alignment. Occasionally, the Caledonian structures introduce a north-east to south-west alignment of forms as in Loch Sunart, Loch Shiel and Glen Affric. Apart from some Tertiary intrusive rocks in Ardnamurchan, some Tertiary lavas in southern Morven and the large mass of granite south of Strontian, the underlying rocks all belong to the Moine metamorphic series and are mainly schists and granulites. The highest ground is in the Glen Shiel and Glen Affric areas with numerous summits over 3,500 feet (1,050 m) (*Fig. 33*). Further south in Moidart, Ardgour and Morven summit altitudes are lower, being generally between 1,500 feet (450 m) and 2,500 feet (750 m).

The mountains of this area may not be rugged and spectacular, but between Glenfinnan and Glenshiel is one of the most complicated pieces of terrain in Scotland (*Fig. 34*). The preglacial landforms probably consisted of a deeply dissected plateau with a watershed quite near to the west coast and with the longest stream flowing to Loch Linnhe. This ridge and valley system became a major centre of ice accumulation during the Pleistocene and valley glaciers expanded both east and west from the line of the old watershed. Eventually, the whole area was completely buried by ice so that ice was able to overflow from one valley to the next by means of low cols and these, in turn, were eroded away by the ice to produce new valleys at right angles to the original valley system. Good examples of this type of valley development are Glen Quoich and Glen Finnan. A close examination of this area also reveals that many of the main valleys do not have corries at their heads, but instead have low cols. Glacial erosion has been so severe that many corrie back walls have been eroded away to provide through-valleys which cut right through old watersheds. The intricate valley network of this area certainly owes very little of its present pattern to the work of the preglacial rivers. The mountain ice cap became so thick and powerful that it established its own centres of dispersal. Some of these were east of the preglacial watershed so that ice flowed westward to cut deep troughs through some of the highest ground.

There are good examples of corries in this area, but many of them are located on north facing slopes above the major west to east through valleys (e.g. the south side of Glen Tarbert and the north side of the Five Sisters Ridge). It is not surprising that this area supported many glaciers during the very last phase of

33. The Five Sisters of Kintail, Glen Shiel.

34. Loch Loyne.

glaciation, about 10,500 years ago. At that time, valley glaciers extended down to the mouths of many of the sea lochs on the west coast. On the east side so much ice existed that it was able to cross the Great Glen and push up Glen Spean and Glen Roy. This part of North-central Scotland contains more deep rock basins cut primarily by glacial erosion than any other part of Scotland. Loch Morar, the deepest loch in Scotland, descends to 987 feet (296 m) below sea level, while Loch Shiel, Loch Arkaig and Loch Quoich are all over 300 feet (90 m) deep. The extension of the glacial troughs and their associated rock basins to the west coast, gives it a very indented character with many classic fiords.

The percentage of low angle slopes and areas of low altitude are very small in this area. Even many of the valley floors are covered with chaotic mounds 20 to 30 feet (6 to 10 m) high left by the wastage of the last valley glaciers. There are limited spreads of sand and gravel, often terraced, along some of the straths and there is a limited development of raised marine platforms and beach deposits along the west coast.

Between Strath Bran and Loch Shin, the east-west alignment of ridges and valleys is not so well-developed and much of the ground is below 2,000 feet (600 m). There are three mountain groups over 3,000 feet (900 m): Sgurr Mor (3,637 feet, 1,091 m), Ben Wyvis (3,433 feet, 1,030 m) and Ben Dearg (3,547 feet, 1,064 m). All three of these areas exhibit clear evidence of severe glacial erosion. It is believed that the ice shed of the last ice sheet was slightly east of the present watershed in the area, so that ice flowed westward out of the Loch Fannich basin and north-westwards from the rolling uplands north-east of Beinn Dearg. Throughout the area the preglacial drainage pattern has been largely destroyed and many through valleys exist. On the high plateau north of Ben Wyvis, the rivers follow very unusual courses as a result of the modification of the valley system by glacial activity. However, the principal preglacial valleys of the Dirrie More, Strath Oykel and Loch Shin were simply made wider and deeper by glacial activity and now form very important routeways to the north-west Highlands.

The landforms north of Loch Shin have two main characteristics: a general alignment of valleys and mountains in a north-north-east to south-south-west direction and a series of isolated mountains which stand above an upland surface between 800 and 1,000 feet (240 and 300 m). The alignment of features largely reflects structures in the Moine schists.

The high ground to the north-west of Loch Shin consists of Moine schists and granulites and Ben Hope (3,040 feet, 1,012 m) with its great, west-facing escarpment is a mountain of unusual dimensions of this type of material. Ben Loyal (2,504 feet, 751 m) is the most easterly of the great northern mountains and it is quite different from all the other Sutherland mountains. It consists of syenite, an igneous intrusive rock, the weathering of which has produced tors and castle-like forms which cause it to be classed as one of Scotland's most impressive mountains.

To the north-east of Loch Shin are Ben Kilbreck (3,154 feet, 946 m) and Ben Armine (2,338 feet, 701 m), both areas coinciding with granite material which has been injected into the Moine schists and granulites. The remainder of the ground north of Loch Shin is characterised by low angle slopes except where the major valleys such as Strath More, Strath Naver and Strath Halladale have been cut into the upland surface. These valleys were major routeways for ice moving north from the various mountain groups already described. The floors of these valleys are filled with glacial and fluviglacial debris in the form of mounds and terraces. The uplands between these valleys show little obvious evidence of glaciation apart from the cover of glacial till which is generally hidden beneath peat.

The North-central Highlands are not so very different to the Grampians. Both regions have a large variety of landforms and there is quite a difference between the complex ridge and valley systems of the southern parts of both regions compared with the more open aspects of their northern parts.

THE ANCIENT FORELAND

The oldest rocks in Scotland occur north-west of the major thrust zone known as the Moine Thrust (*Fig. 6*). This line of thrusting, which can be clearly traced from Loch Eriboll to the Sound of Sleat, makes a distinct break in the geology and landforms of the Northern Highlands. To the north-west of this line, the closely spaced ridges and valleys that characterise the remainder of the Highland mainland are replaced either by intensely glaciated lowlands or low plateaus of metamorphic rock, or relatively isolated mountains of Torridonian sandstone. The solid geology of the north-west mainland is very similar to that of the Outer Hebridean islands except that the latter have only a very small outcrop of the Torridonian sandstone cover. There is some evidence to indicate that the metamorphic rocks of North and South Uist are very similar to those of the mainland between Loch Laxford and Little Loch Broom. If these areas of similar rock type and structure are plotted on a map, their distribution implies that, relative to the mainland, the whole of the Long Island has moved south-westwards in relation to the mainland along a tear fault like that in the Great Glen. It is probable that prior to the development of the trough now occupied by the Minch, an ancient land mass of metamorphic rock occupied the area now known as North-west Scotland. It has become known as the ancient foreland because of its great age and because it was against this rock mass that the younger rocks to the south-east were pushed to produce the characteristic Caledonian structures.

There can be little doubt that the North-west Highlands can claim to have the most dramatic and varied scenery of any part of the Highlands and Islands. There are essentially three landform types: very rough, mammilated surfaces developed on Lewisian gneiss; massive mountains of Torridonian sandstone; complicated mountain and valley systems associated with the earth movements along the Moine Thrust.

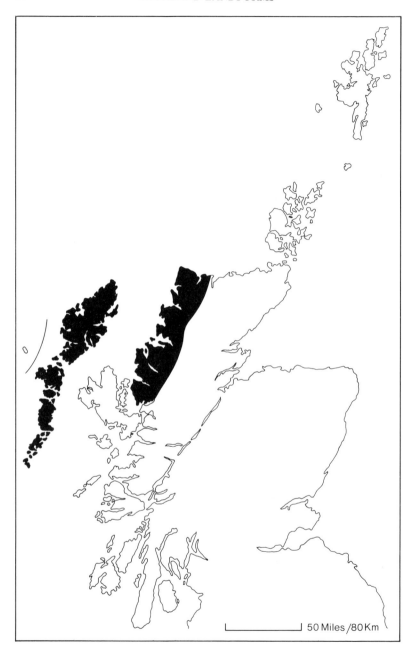

Map C.   The Ancient Foreland.

Although Lewisian gneiss probably underlies the whole of the North-west Highlands, extensive outcrops occur only in three localities: between Cape Wrath and Enard Bay; between Gruinard Bay and Loch Gairloch, and between Loch Carron and Loch Hourn. The characteristic forms of the areas of gneiss are numerous ridges and mounds of bare rock separated by peat-filled or lake-filled hollows. Most of the land is between 300 feet (90 m) and 800 feet (240 m) in altitude with relative relief values of 50 to 300 feet (15 to 90 m). The main structures in the ancient foreland are aligned west-north-west to east-south-east and their influence is clearly seen in the alignment of many sea lochs, valleys and ridges. The mammilated surface of the gneiss is primarily the result of intensive glacial erosion by ice moving west and north-west from the high ground along the line of Moine Thrust.

Resting unconformably on top of the Lewisian gneiss are the remains of a once much more extensive cover of Torridonian sandstone. Large areas of the sandstone outcrop between Loch Kishorn and Enard Bay and north of Loch Inchard. The Torridonian sandstone is well-bedded and jointed so that the results of weathering and erosion have produced striking landforms. Vertical faces, massive crags and stepped hill-sides are common features. These ancient sandstones form some of the most spectacular mountain scenery in Scotland. There are many mountains between 2,500 feet (750 m) and 3,400 feet (1,020 m) between Loch Carron and Loch Broom which consist primarily of Torridonian sandstone (*Fig. 35*) although some of them have relatively thin caps of Cambrian quartzite. Perhaps the most spectacular members of the group are Beinn Eighe (3,309 feet, 993 m) and An Teallach (3,484 feet, 1045 m).

The deep dissection of the sandstones by rivers and ice has produced an intricate landform pattern. Deep, straight, glacial troughs such as Coire Dubh, south of Beinn Eighe, or Glen Docherty (*Fig. 36*), or the low level pass between Kinlochewe and Upper Loch Torridon, are good examples of the severity of glacial erosion. There are also excellent examples of high level corries in the area with Loch Coire on the north side of Beinn Eighe perhaps being the finest.

The Torridonian mountains south of Loch Broom are rather different from those further north. Although deeply dissected, the sandstone forming the southern group is part of a fairly continuous cover which has not been removed to reveal the underlying

35. Ben Eighe.

36. Glen Docharty and Loch Maree.

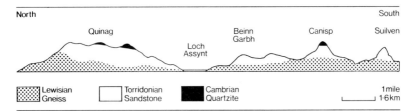

37. A geological section from north to south in Sutherland.

Lewisian gneiss. To the north of Loch Broom, apart from the Coigach area, the Torridonian has been largely removed to leave only limited outcrops which stand up above the Lewisian gneiss to form the most spectacular mountains in Scotland (*Figs 37, 38*). Stac Pollaidh (2,009 feet, 603 m), Cul Mor (2,787 feet, 836 m), Suilven (2,399 feet, 720 m), Canisp (2,779 feet, 834 m), Quinag (2,651 feet, 795 m) and Ben Stac (2,356 feet, 706 m), although not the highest mountains in Scotland, rise quickly and steeply from the mammilated surface of the surrounding Lewisian gneiss which rarely reaches altitudes above 600 feet (180 m). Some of these peaks have cappings of Cambrian quartzite (e.g. Quinag and Canisp). The isolated peaks of Suilven, Canisp and Stac Pollaidh do not exhibit

38. Suilven, Canisp, Cul Mor.

well-developed features of glacial erosion. This is probably because they did not have sufficient ground at high altitude to nourish their own corrie glaciers. Quinag, Cul Mor and the Coigach Mountains on the other hand do contain well-developed corries. The whole of the area was overrun by ice which originated within or east of the belt of high ground stretching from Cranstakie (2,630 feet, 789 m) in the north through Ben More Assynt (3,273 feet, 982 m), Beinn Dearg (3,547 feet, 1,064 m) and the Fannich Mountains.

There remains one further group of landforms in the North-west Highlands which must be discussed. So far the landforms of this region have consisted of what is usually referred to as the foreland: the relatively stable and ancient basement of gneiss and its covering of Torridonian sandstone. This foreland is terminated on its eastern margin by a series of thrust plains or low angle faults along which Moine schists and Cambrian and Ordovician sediments have moved north-westwards across the stable foreland for distances of 8–12 miles (12–19 km). This relatively narrow zone of complicated structures and varying lithologies has distinctive landforms in the shape of a series of westward facing escarpments associated with the various thrust planes and the outcrops of Cambrian quatzites and limestones. Three mountains, Cranstackie (2,630 feet, 789 m), Foinaven (2,980 feet, 894 m) and Arkle (2,486 feet, 745 m) consist of Cambrian quartzite and limestone and each has very steep west facing slopes, with more gentle eastern slopes which have been cut into by large corries. In particular, the north-east side of Fionaven has been cut into by three large corries, one of which has two distinct levels.

In the region of Ben More Assynt (3,273 feet, 982 m) the width of the outcrop of the Cambrian sediments and the area affected by the various thrust planes is much wider. This results in an area of very complex geology and a series of mountains and valleys of consider-able size and interest. There is a strong, north-west to south-east alignment of valleys and the steeper slopes are west facing. There are considerable areas of low angle slopes associated with Cam-brian limestones with gentle dips. The whole area was intensively glaciated and there are some excellent corries.

South of Ullapool the outcrop of Cambrian sediments is quite narrow and the effect of the Moine thrust (and associated thrusts) on landform development is not very marked. Only in the Beinn Eighe district do the Cambrian sediments again become important elements in landform development.

Each of the mountain groups in the North-west Highlands shoes strong evidence of glacial activity. In the early phases of the development of the last ice sheet each group would have acted as a centre for ice accumulation and dispersal. At the maximum stage of the glaciation the ice was so thick that movement was able to take place from east to west across the preglacial watershed. The dominant line of movement, in fact, was north-westwards and this allowed the cutting of the many 'through valleys' such as the valley which now contains Loch More and Loch Merkland (the route of the A38 road), the series of valleys followed by the A837 road, the Dirrie More at the head of Loch Broom and the valleys between Achnasheen and Kinlochewe. So much ice accumulated in the north-west Highlands that it was able to fill the Minch and proceed north-westwards across the Isle of Lewis and out into the floor of the Atlantic.

The ancient foreland is continued in the islands of the Outer Hebrides which, apart from St Kilda, consist primarily of Lewisian gneiss, a metamorphic rock over 2,000 million years old, although some granite occurs in North and South Harris. The Outer Hebrides stretch for a distance of some 150 miles (250 km) along the west Highland coast and are exposed to the full force of the Atlantic waves and weather. Apart from south-west Lewis, Harris and eastern South Uist, most of the land is below 400 feet (120 m) and there are extensive areas below 100 feet (30 m). In many ways it is misleading to write about the landforms of the Outer Hebrides as water is everywhere dominant in the form of hundreds of lakes and a greatly indented coastline which is always near at hand. Most of the islands are long and narrow and rarely is any land more than 5 miles (8 km) from the sea. Even on Lewis which has a maximum width of 30 miles (48 km), because of the many indentations in the coastline, there is very little land further than 8 miles (13 km) from the sea.

Lewis and Harris would in fact be two islands but for a neck of land less than half a mile (0.8 km) wide and less than 50 feet (15 m) above sea level. Lewis consists mainly of a rolling upland with the highest ground along a central backbone attaining heights of between 700 feet (210 m) and 800 feet (248 m). In many ways Lewis appears to be an ancient land surface with residual hills (e.g. Beinn Mholach and Muirneag) standing above the general level. Just how ancient this surface is, is not known as there is no record of the geological events which have occurred in this area since the

metamorphism of the Lewisian gneiss. The last touches were given
to this northern upland by glacial ice which crossed the Minch from
the mainland. The ice did not achieve a great deal of erosion but it
did deposit till of variable thickness.

There is a striking contrast between the rolling upland of
northern Lewis and the rugged mountains of south Lewis and
Harris. Between the mountains and the upland there is a basin with
extensive development of knob and lochan landscape. The mountain area is in part associated with masses of granite although the
highest peak, Clisham (2,622 feet, 787 m) consists of gneiss. These
mountains were a centre for local ice accumulation and corries,
deep troughs and over-steepened valley sides are common. Local
relief values of between 1,000 feet (300 m) and 1,500 feet (450 m)
are quite common. Ice moving northwards from these mountains
met north-westerly flowing ice from the mainland. The lowland,
north of the mountains, experienced very severe erosion. The
alignment of many rock basins, through valleys and ridges, clearly
indicates the tendency of glacial erosion to pick out the major
structural grain which, in this area, is from north-north-west to
south-south-east.

South Harris contains a considerable amount of high ground with
several rounded summits of 1,000 feet (300 m) and 1,500 feet (450
m). However, it is the eastern coastal strip of south Harris which
contains some impressive landforms. This coastal strip of Lewisian
gneiss is generally below 200 feet (60 m) in altitude but it has been
intensively eroded by glacial ice to produce a very irregular surface
of steepsided ridges and hummocks separated by peat-filled or
water-filled depressions. The local relief rarely exceeds 100 feet (30
m) but these landforms contribute to one of the most inhospitable
landscapes in the Highlands and Islands.

North Uist, Benbecula and South Uist – the three islands linked
by causeways – are all underlain by Lewisian Gneiss which has
strong north-north-west to south-south-east structural trend.
Apart from Marrival (757 feet, 227 m) on North Uist, all the high
ground occurs on the eastern side of the islands and rounded hills
attain altitudes of between 800 feet (240 m) and 2,000 feet (600 m).
These hills drop quite steeply to the east coast while there is a more
gentle slope westwards providing a drift-covered rock platform
between the coastline and about 200 feet (60 m) above sea level.
Excluding the upland areas, these islands are characterised by two
landform types. There are extensive areas on all three islands

where land and water rapidly alternate either in the form of large numbers of irregularly shaped lakes or in the form of closely spaced islands. Sea lochs such as Loch Eport, Loch Skipport and Loch Eynort almost extend from the east to the west coast. The second landform type is the machair of the west coast which consists of blown sand on top of solid rock or glacial deposits.

The large number of lakes on these islands result from glacial erosion and deposition on a pre-existing rock surface of low relief. The ice from the mainland cross the Minch, over-topped the high ground on the east side of the islands and moved westwards out into the Atlantic. A certain amount of erosion took place on the lower ground to form shallow depressions separated by low mounds, many of which have a capping of glacial till. This landscape is best developed in the eastern half of North Uist. In the north-east of the island these same forms have been drowned by the sea to produce dozens of small islands and inlets.

The machair landforms which dominate the west coast of these islands are also related to the events associated with glaciation, although the nature of the offshore conditions are primarily responsible for the distribution of machair forms. The glaciers which crossed the Minch were forced to climb a steep slope on the east side of the islands but having climbed up on to the east coast and crossed the eastern uplands on to the western platform, they continued westward across a gently sloping offshore platform for some three miles (5 km). The main effect of glaication was the deposition of large quantities of debris on the platform which were subsequently re-worked landwards by coastal processes during the period of rising sea level in post glacial times. This resulted in large amounts of sand and shingle being moved inland to produce the beaches and machair of the Atlantic coast.

The oldest rocks in Scotland, both on the mainland and in the Outer Hebrides, provide a variety of landforms that are the basis of a harsh landscape which has given man very little encouragement in his utilisation of the land. This part of Scotland has remained comparatively distinctive. The limited road network and the necessity for ferries has resulted in the land areas around the Minch having a degree of isolation not found anywhere else on the mainland. The dominance of bare rock, both on lowlands and in the mountains of the ancient foreland, makes this region quite different from the rest of the Highlands and Islands.

THE NORTH-EAST HIGHLANDS, ORKNEY AND SHETLAND

North of the Great Glen fault the mountains of the North Central Highlands give way eastwards to a more gentle and more open landscape. There is no sudden transformation between the two regions. East of Strath Naver and south-east of Ben Armine, the closely spaced ridges and valleys of the North Central Highlands are replaced by a rolling upland generally between 600 feet (200 m) and 1,000 feet (300 m) above sea level. Wide, shallow valleys in the upland either lead northwards or south-eastwards. This upland is underlain by the same metamorphic rocks that form the mountains of the North Central Highlands but here they have not been so deeply dissected.

East of Strath Halladale, there are large outcrops of granite which form rounded hills that attain altitudes of between 600 feet (180 m) and 1,200 feet (360 m) along the Caithness and Sutherland boundary. The remainder of Caithness consists of a rolling landscape nearly everywhere below 600 feet (180 m) and underlain by sandstones of Old Red Sandstone age. Very wide valleys, bounded by gentle slopes and separated by broad low divides, produce a landscape quite different from any other part of the Highlands and Islands. In fact it is very misleading to refer to this region as 'Highland'. The rolling landscape developed on the Caithness sandstones is continued in Orkney, but Shetland is made quite different from the rest of the region by the reappearance of metamorphic rocks.

Around the shores of the Moray, Beauly, Cromarty and Dornoch Firths, sandstones similar to those which outcrop in Caithness, provide a coastal zone of lower altitude backed by low mountains with rounded summits between 1,000 feet (300 m) and 1,500 feet (450 m). The valleys leading down to the firths are characterised by wide terraces cut in fluvioglacial sands and gravels

Map D.   The North-East Highlands, Orkney and Shetland.

while the coastal areas have fine examples of raised beaches.

Between Golspie and Helmsdale there is a narrow outcrop of Jurassic sediments. This is backed by a series of rounded summits between 1,200 feet (360 m) and 2,000 feet (600 m) which are at the southern extremity of a belt of high ground extending some five miles on either side of the Caithness–Sutherland boundary. Slopes are gentle and rounded, for the most part, as the hills are developed on granite or sandstone. The steeper slopes of Morven (2,313 feet, 694 m) and Maiden Pap (1,587 feet, 576 m) are formed of conglomerates while Scaraben (2,054 feet, 616 m) is formed of quartzite.

The Old Red Sandstone rocks around the shores of the Moray Firth and in Caithness provide the most extensive areas of low altitude (i.e. below 400 feet, 120 m) anywhere in the Highlands. These bedded sandstones have been eroded by rivers and ice to produce the least dramatic landforms of the Highland mainland. Wide, shallow valleys and low divides are aligned either north to south or north-west to south-east to form a landscape more akin to a low plateau (*Fig. 39*), contrasting with the mountains which dominate the rest of the Highland mainland.

There is a general decrease in altitude from west to east in Caithness with the higher ground underlain mainly by conglomerates and sandstone and the lower ground by flagstones. The flagstones are very well-bedded sandstones traditionally and extensively used as building materials. Although there is considerable variation in the lithology and structure of the Old Red Sandstone rocks of Caithness this has not produced marked differences in landform development on the plateau. Nevertheless, variations in the coastal plan and profile are frequently the result of local variations in lithology and the effects of faulting, folding or jointing. Perhaps of most importance is the angle of the dip of the beds of sandstone when they reach the coast.

The direct evidence of glaciation in the area is not great. The source areas for all the ice to cover the north-east Highlands were outside the area itself. Ice originating in the North Central Highlands flowed eastwards down Strath Farrar, Glen Orrin and Strath Conon and was joined by ice moving south-eastwards from Ben Wyvis and down Strathcarron and Strath Fleet so that the Moray, Cromarty and Dornoch Firths became filled with a north-easterly flowing ice stream. Further north the high ground of eastern Sutherland was the source of ice which moved eastwards

39. The Caithness plateau.

40. The Orkney mainland.

and north-eastwards towards Caithness. Nearly all of Caithness, however, was overwhelmed by ice from the south-east. The ice moving north-eastwards out of the Moray Firth was turned back on to the land by the presence of ice which had crossed the North Sea from Scandinavia. The southern origin of the ice which crossed Caithness is proved by the presence of marine shells in the till and by the presence of fragments of Mesozoic rock which were derived from the off-shore zone. The ice sheet which covered Caithness did not create many new landforms. There is little evidence of intensive glacial erosion and the main contribution of glacial activity was to fill the pre-existing hollows and valleys with till. The till is thin on the higher ground, but is quite thick in valleys and hollows. Along the coastline, the red-brown till caps most of the cliffs and forms cliffs in its own right in a few places, notably at Scrabster.

The Orkney Islands continue the sandstone landforms of Caithness on the far side of the Pentland Firth. There are some ninety islands and skerries in the group and apart from a very small area of granite and schistose rocks near Stromness and limited outcrops of igneous material, the islands are formed by flagstone and sandstones of Old Red Sandstone age. The island of Hoy stands out in marked contrast to the other members of the group. On Hoy, hills with steep but rounded outlines reach altitudes of between 1,000 feet (300 m) and 1,500 feet (450 m) whereas all the other islands have only very small areas above 600 feet (180 m).

Throughout the Orkneys there is an impression of a very old landscape with remnant hills and wide open valleys which have been truncated by the coastline (*Fig. 40*). The present land area is undoubtedly a remnant of a much more extensive landmass. If sea level dropped about 120 feet (36 m) the present individual islands would form one island. Although there is evidence of relatively recent drowning of the land – that is over the last 10,000 years – the history of formation of this island group is only partially understood. The rolling hills and open valleys were presumably formed at a time when a drainage system had developed on the formerly more extensive land area. At what stage the Orkney Islands became a separate entity and the sea invaded the lower area is not known.

During glaciation, ice from the Scottish mainland was deflected by Scandinavian ice so that the Scottish ice was pushed north-westwards across the Orkney Islands. The main effect of glaciation was the deposition of till which, in places, contains fragments of sea shells derived from the sea floor across which the ice moved. The till deposits thin out up slopes but are thicker on the floors of the valleys. The island of Hoy may well have nourished its own glaciers at both an early stage and late stage of glaciation. Glacial troughs and corries are quite well-developed in north Hoy and the floors of the troughs contain morainic mounds and fluvioglacial sands and gravels. Apart from Hoy, the Orkney Islands do not exhibit strong evidence of glaciation.

The Shetland Islands lie some fifty miles north-north-east of Orkney and, although Fair Isle, Foula, the west and south-east Mainland and Bressay consist of sandstone and have similar landforms as the Orkney Islands, the remainder of Shetland consists of a highly diversified series of metamorphic and igneous rocks. The strong north to south alignment of the structures in the metamorphic rocks is expressed in the alignment of the Mainland, Yell and Unst. Granite underlies much of North Roe and forms the rounded Ronas Hill (1,425 feet, 427 m) which is the highest point in Shetland. The metamorphic rocks on the Mainland have been strongly folded, and the erosion of relatively hard and soft bands within the system have produced a series of en écholon ridges and valleys with the ridges attaining altitudes of between 600 and 900 feet (180 and 270 m). Similar but smaller ridges form the backbones of Unst and Yell. The slopes on some of these ridges are quite steep but most forms are well rounded and the rugged character of much of the metamorphic area of the Scottish mainland is not found in Shetland.

There is little evidence of severe glacial erosion except in the form of the deep, fiord-like re-entrants such as Ronas Voe, Dales Voe and Weisdale Voe. The Shetlands are believed to have nourished their own glaciers at an early stage of glaciation, but with the expansion of the Scandinavian ice sheet across the floor of the North Sea they were invaded by Scandinavian ice from the south-south-east.

The landforms of the Orkney and Shetland Islands are not in themselves very exciting compared with the Highland mainland. However, it is in their coastal landforms that they excel. A great variety of forms occur within both island groups but these will be discussed in the section on coastal landforms.

ARRAN, THE INNER HEBRIDES AND ST KILDA

In the Scottish Census Report of 1861 an island was defined as 'any piece of land surrounded by water, which affords sufficient vegetation to support one or more sheep or which is inhabited by man'. By this definition there are 787 Scottish islands and of these over 500 are located off the west Highland coastline. The Western Isles are divided by the Minch into two groups, the Inner and Outer Hebrides. The islands of the Inner Hebrides can be divided into two groups according to their geology. Islay, Jura, Colonsay, Tiree and Coll consist of ancient metamorphic rocks while Skye, Canna, Rhum, Eigg, Muck and Mull consist largely of volcanic rocks of Tertiary age. The islands of Arran and St Kilda are also discussed in this section because they, too, were greatly affected by the Tertiary volcanic activity.

Islay is the most southerly of the Inner Hebrides. The eastern half of the island is underlain by Dalradian quartzites, schists and limestones which form rounded uplands rising to 1,600 feet (480 m). The dominant north-east to south-west trend of the Dalradian rocks once again affects the alignment of landforms. The western half of the island is underlain by Torridonian sandstones and grits with an outcrop of Lewisian gneiss forming the Rhinns of Islay. The landforms in the west are quite subdued with most of the land below 700 feet (210 m). The irregularities in the shape of Islay's coastline largely reflect the differential resistance to erosion of the various rock types on the island. On the west coast there are several deep embayments and nearly a quarter of the island's coastline has sandy beaches. Islay does not exhibit many features of strong glacial erosion although it was overridden by ice moving south-westwards from the mainland. As an indirect result of former glaciation there are raised beaches and fossil cliffs well-developed between Loch Indaal and Loch Gruinart and around Saligo Bay.

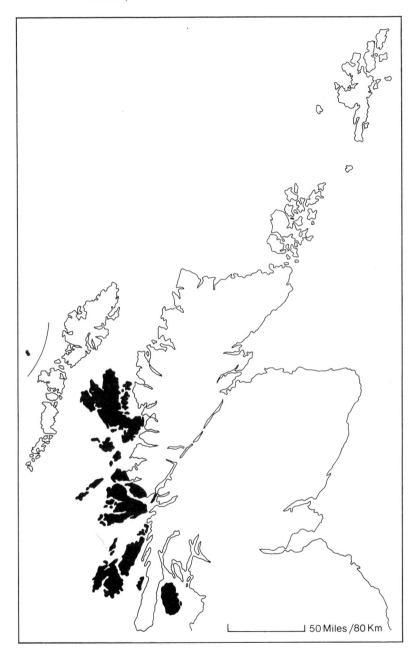

Map E. Arran, the Inner Hebrides and St Kilda.

Islay is separated from Jura by a narrow but deep sound and the Dalradian quartzites of south east Islay continue northwards to form the high backbone of Jura. These quartzites have resisted erosion and there are extensive uplands over 1,000 feet (300 m) with the Paps of Jura rising to over 2,400 feet (720 m). There is only a relatively small amount of low ground but the highest ground in the south east shows strong evidence of glaciation with well-developed corries and troughs.

It is Jura's coastal landforms which are of greatest interest. The characteristic coastline consists of a zone up to half a mile (0.8 km) wide formed by a series of elevated marine platforms upon which rest deposits of earlier, higher sea levels. The abandoned cliffs, caves and sea stacks, along with the platforms and deposits, are so well-developed along the west coast of Jura that this entire coastline has been designated a site of special scientific interest by the Nature Conservancy Council. There is much debate about the age of these features but it is likely that some of the higher and older platforms pre-date the last glaciation and may be even older.

Colonsay and Oronsay, which are separated only by the tide, are situated some 8 miles (13 km) to the west of Jura and consist of Torridonian sandstones and mudstones. These islands represent the remains of a dissected plateau with very little ground over 300 feet (90 m). Several shallow, open valleys cross them from east-north-east to west-south-west. Glacial ice from the mainland overran the islands but there is no spectacular evidence of glacial erosion. There are good examples of raised marine features around Kiloran Bay in the north and south of Scalasaig. Both islands contain large areas of blown sand, particularly on the west and south west. Throughout the Hebrides these blown sand areas are known as machair and often provide the best soils for cultivation and pasture.

There are only two other islands in the Inner Hebrides which are not dominated by Tertiary igneous rocks – Coll and Tiree. They consist almost entirely of Lewisian gneiss which makes them very similar to the islands of the Outer Hebrides. Both islands are low in altitude, below 200 feet (60 m), with a subdued topography. The coastline is irregular with embayments backed by sandy beaches and machair.

The remaining islands in the Inner Hebrides along with Arran and St Kilda were all affected by great volcanic activity which took place during the Tertiary period. Areas of older rocks also occur on

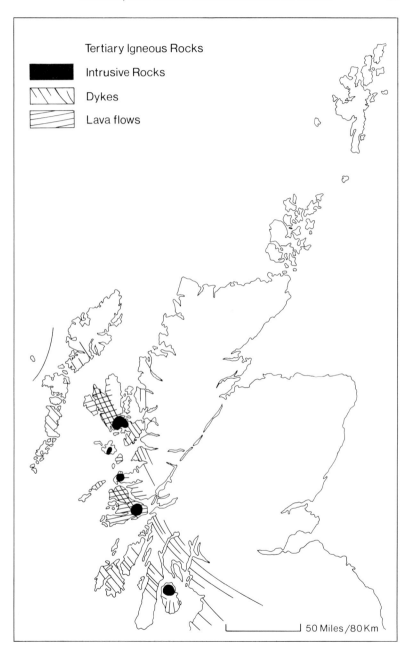

Tertiary Igneous Rocks

Intrusive Rocks

Dykes

Lava flows

50 Miles/80 Km

41. Map of the Tertiary volcanic centres and dyke swarms.

these islands but, most of their present landforms are related to lavas or intrusive igneous rock.

The volcanicity of 60 million years ago had two main phases. Firstly, there was a long period during which lavas poured out of fissures in the earth's crust in flows 20 feet (6 m) to 100 feet (30 m) thick and piled up to attain a total thickness of several thousand feet. These lavas formed a tableland of which northern Skye, the Small Isles and Mull now represent much dissected remnants. The lava phase was followed by the upwelling of magma which either solidified just below the earth's surface or which exploded through the crust to form great volcanoes on the surface. The intrusion of great masses of granite and gabbro and the development of volcanoes was accompanied by a fracturing of the earth's crust and from each volcanic or intrusive centre linear dykes were intruded (*Fig. 41*). For example, dykes associated with the Mull volcanic centre follow a general north-west to south-east trend and cut through the older rocks of Lorn, Cowal, the Glasgow area and even extend into England. These dykes were not the feeders for the great lava piles but post date them. Depending on whether the dyke material is harder or softer than the material into which it was intruded the location of a dyke is marked either by a ridge or a depression, usually 3–12 feet (0.9–3.6 m) wide. They are often best observed on coastal rock platforms. The basalt lava flows formed a massive plateau topped in places by volcanic cones. Erosion has been so great during the later part of the Tertiary and Pleistocene periods that only the roots of the volcanoes remain. Much of the highest ground is now formed by the exposed masses of granite and gabbro of the cores of the volcanoes revealed by the removal of great thicknesses of basalt.

The island of Arran contains a wide variety of geology and landforms in its area of 430 sq km. Only 20 miles (60 km) from north to south it contains rocks ranging in age from pre-Cambrian to Tertiary and exhibits many of the classic features of glaciation. It has a fairly regular coastline with few embayments except for Loch Ranza, Brodick and Lamlash Bays. There are well-developed cliffs at Bennan Head but elsewhere the coast is bordered by a narrow strip of raised beaches often backed by a fossil cliff a short distance inland.

Arran can be divided into two parts. The southern half of the island consists of uplands rising only to 1,800 feet (550 m) in the north and only 1,000 feet (300 m) in the south where there is a steep descent to the coast. The western side of the upland consists of long rounded spurs while the eastern side is dissected by short deeply-incised valleys. The northern half of the island is very different. It is much higher, rising to 2,910 feet (873 m) in Goatfell (*Fig. 42*) and generally much more rugged. There is an abundance of Alpine forms which combine to produce a spectacular landscape. The mountains rise abruptly from an upland surface at between 1,000 feet (300 m) and 1,500 feet (450 m). There is very little lowland in the north of the island, the only exceptions being where valleys reach the coast and the narrow fringe of raised beach.

The contrast between the northern and southern halfs of Arran is basically a result of geological history. The southern half of the island is underlain by Permian, Triassic, Jurassic, Cretaceous and Tertiary sediments and lavas while the northern half of the island is dominated by Tertiary granites surrounded by pre-Cambrian schists. It is the granites which form the highest ground.

The island forms part of the Tertiary volcanic district which extended from Northern Ireland to Iceland via the Faroes. Throughout that district great piles of lava were extruded on to the surface and great masses of granite were intruded. Unlike Mull and

42.   Goat Fell, Arran.

Skye, Arran does not exhibit great lava piles, only the granite masses and numerous sills and dykes. The granites, dykes and sills occupy 42 per cent of the total surface area of the island and the granites have been dated at over 60 million years old. It is out of this granite that the high peaks, the serrated ridges and the massive buttresses of the northern mountains have been carved. Even though the present mountains are impressive they represent only the roots of a much more massive mountain system built up during the Tertiary period and which has been severely eroded. There is virtually no evidence of the nature of this erosion. The drainage pattern now seen on Arran has been greatly modified by glaciation and the relationship of the river valleys on the island to the river system on the mainland can only be guessed at.

The northern mountains of Arran were high enough to develop their own ice cap during the onset of glaciation. The first glaciers to develop established a radial pattern of movement but as the mainland ice sheet developed, these local glaciers were over-whelmed by ice moving southwards from the south-west Grampians. Kilbrannan Sound and the Firth of Clyde were filled with ice and the main movement of ice on Arran at the maximum of the ice sheet was from north to south or north-east to south-west. Since the last ice sheet melted away about 13,000 years ago, the southern half of the island has remained ice free but the northern mountains nourished local glaciers about 10,500 years ago and these glaciers descended to about 500 feet (150 m).

Arran has a great deal to offer the student of rocks and landforms. There is no other part of the Highlands and Islands where such a range of rock types and landforms can be examined in such a small area.

The irregularly shaped island of Mull is separated from Morven by the narrow Sound of Mull and from Lorn by the Firth of Lorn. The island can be divided into two distinct parts on the basis of rock type. The south eastern part of Mull is dominated by intrusive igneous rocks (e.g. gabbro, granite and felsite) and once again they represent the roots of a formerly much more extensive volcanic pile. These rocks have been severely eroded by rivers and glaciers so that peaks between 2,300 feet (690 m) and 3,169 feet (950 m) are separated by deep valleys. Apart from the western end of the Ross of Mull, which consists of schist and granite, the rest of the island is underlain by Tertiary lava flows resulting in a 'stepped' landscape with considerable areas between 1,000 feet (300 m) and 1,400 feet (420 m).

During the build up of the last Scottish ice sheet, the mountains of south eastern Mull almost certainly would have developed their own glaciers at an early stage but with the expansion of the mainland ice sheet, ice moving down Loch Linnhe was pushed westwards by ice moving out of Loch Etive. Eventually Mull became overridden by ice originating on the mainland and which was moving west and south-west across the island. After the disappearance of the last ice sheet small valley glaciers developed on Mull about 10,500 years ago. They descended down to the coast in Glen Forsa, at the mouth of Loch Ba, to the head of Loch Scridain and the mouth of Loch Spelve.

Rhum is composed of Pre-Cambrian Torridonian rocks through which a suite of igneous rocks was thrust in early Tertiary times. The Torridonian rocks occur primarily to the north of Kinloch Glen where these sediments dip at angles mainly between 20° and 25° to the north-west. The more resistant members of the Torridonian sediments tend to form small scarps so that the northern part of the island tends to have an uninviting appearance resulting from a stepped landscape formed by numerous small cliffs.

The southern two-thirds of Rhum consist of intrusive igneous rocks which can be divided into two geological and topographical units. The western part consists largely of granophyre, an acid plutonic rock, which forms a rolling upland most of which is below 1,500 feet (450 m). The eastern part consists predominantly of basic igneous rocks (e.g. peridotite and eucrite). This area is sometimes called the Rhum Cuillin as it is characterised by a series of mountains, Askival 2,663 feet (799 m), Hallival 2,365 feet (709 m) and Trollaval 2,300 feet (690 m) all of which have been eaten into by glacial erosion to produce pointed summits, narrow ridges and steep corrie walls (*Fig. 43*). Even though the rocks forming the Rhum Cuillin are not very resistant to erosion they still form the highest ground because it is believed that they were uplifted as much as 7,000 feet (2,100 m) at the time of the Tertiary volcanic activity and even after the subsequent severe erosion they still form mountains. Much of the lava associated with the vulcanism has been eroded away but a whole series of dykes, consisting mainly of dolerite, radiate outwards from Glen Harris. Over 700 of these dykes have been recorded.

Like Mull, Rhum probably nourished its own glaciers at first but was eventually overrun by mainland ice. Great streams of ice flowed in troughs between Rhum and Skye, between Rhum and

43. The Rhum Cuillin.

Canna – where there is a trough over 700 feet (210 m) deep – and between Rhum and Eigg. After the disappearance of the ice sheet, corrie glaciers developed at the heads of the glens in the southern part of the island. An indication of the continued severity of the climate on the higher summits of Rhum is the occurrence of deposits and forms which are produced by alternating freezing and thawing of surface materials. Periglacial features such as block fields and solifluction terraces occur on Orval. On the tops of Barkival, Hallival, Askival and Trollaval there is evidence of severe frost action in the form of solifluction debris, screes, tors, solifluction terraces, stone polygons and stripes.

The islands of Canna, Eigg and Muck consist almost entirely of Tertiary lavas. They are characterised by a series of steps often rising from steep, cliffed coastlines to altitudes up to 400 feet (120 m); on Eigg the Sgurr rises to 1,289 feet (387 m).

Skye is the largest island of the Inner Hebrides. It has a very irregular shape with numerous long peninsulas separated by deep sounds or sea lochs. The island consists primarily of Tertiary igneous rocks except for the Sleat peninsula which consists of Pre-Cambrian rocks and two areas of Mesozoic sediments – one between Broadford and Suisnish, the other extending along the east and north sides of the Trotternish peninsula. The high ground at the northern end of the Sleat peninsula is underlain by Torridonian sandstone and although the sandstone continues to form the backbone of this peninsula it is bordered to the west by Moine schist and to the east by Lewisian gneiss.

Broadford Bay is cut into Jurassic shales and sandstones but the higher ground to the south of Broadford is formed of volcanic rocks. Between the granites of Beinn an Dubhaich and Beinn na Caillach there is an outcrop of Durness limestone which reaches the west coast at Torrin.

The most impressive landforms of Skye are associated with intrusive volcanic rocks which form the basis of the Cuillin Hills (*Fig. 44*) and Red Hills (*Fig. 45*). The Cuillins consist mainly of gabbro with some dolerite, peridotite and agglomerate whereas the Red Hills consist mainly of granite and granophyre. The Cuillin Hills are much more rugged and this is largely because of the occurrence of numerous magmatic dykes within the tougher gabbro of the Cuillins. These dykes often weather out to leave gullies and notches.

The Cuillins contain some fine examples of glacial landforms. Many of the rugged peaks and ridges are over 3,000 feet (900 m) and they stand above steep-sided corries (e.g. Coir an Lochain) and glacial troughs (e.g. Loch Coruisk). The steep rock faces produced by glacial action are a great attraction to mountaineers. East of Glen Sligachan the granites of the Red Hills are a little less spectacular with the highest altitudes being between 2,000 feet (600 m) and 2,500 feet (750 m). Evidence of glacial erosion is again strong particularly in the form of Strath Mar, much of the floor of which is only 50 feet (15 m) above sea level.

The Cuillin and Red Hills were a major centre of ice accumulation. Ice moved outwards in all directions from the high ground diverting ice moving off the mainland, via Loch Hourn and the Sound of Sleat, south-westwards towards Rhum. It also diverted ice coming from Loch Alsh and Loch Carron northwards over Raasay.

The northern two-thirds of Skye, apart from the eastern and northern margins of the Trotternish peninsula, consist entirely of plateau lavas. There are many similarities in geology and landforms between Mull and Skye in that both have centres of intrusive and volcanic igneous activity in the south and great accumulations of lavas in the north. On Skye, these lavas cover over 400 square miles

44.   The Cuillins Skye.

45.   Red Hills, Skye.

and are typified by table-topped hills and hillsides terraced as a result of erosion of the lava flows. The present total thickness of these lava flows is over 2,000 feet (600 m). In the north-west the stepped surface attains altitudes of over 1,500 feet (450 m) and in Trotternish the eastern margin of the lavas attains altitudes over 2,000 feet (600 m) before terminating in a dramatic escarpment above Mesozoic sediments. The escarpment in eastern Trotternish exhibits excellent examples of land slips where great masses of basalt have slipped over underlying Jurassic sediments to create very irregular topography. The best example of these landslips is to be seen at the Storr (*Fig. 46*) some six miles (10 km) north of Portree.

The smaller islands around Skye exhibit quite a wide variety of rock types and landforms. Soay and Scalpay consist largely of Torridonian sandstone, while Raasay contains Lewisian gneiss, Torridonian sandstone, Jurassic sediments and Tertiary granite.

The Inner Hebrides are full of variety. They contain rocks of widely differing ages and materials resulting in a variety of landforms. Everywhere glaciation has had a marked effect on the present form of the land and changes of sea level over the past 12,000 years have left relit marine features above the present shoreline. Throughout these islands it is these raised coastal

46. Old Man of Storr, Sky, a landslip.

platforms which often provide routeways and settlement sites. The best soils are found on the raised beaches, on machair sands and fluvioglacial sands and gravels on the valley floors. The centres of Tertiary igneous activity on Mull, Rhum and Skye provide the best mountain scenery while the associated plateau lavas give a distinctive moorland landscape.

There remains one further island group which, although small, is of particular interest in terms of its landforms. St Kilda lies some fifty miles (80 km) west of the Isle of Lewis and is part of the Tertiary volcanic group. The gabbro and granite of St Kilda have been deeply eroded by marine processes so that the main island which is only two miles (3 km) wide has some spectacular cliffs. The summits of the main island, Hirta, are all around a thousand feet (300 m) but their forms are quite different depending on the nature of the underlying rock. The granite of Conachair and Oiseval are smooth paps while the gabbro of Mullach Bi and the smaller islands of Dun, Soay and Boreray are rugged ridges. The magnificent granite cliffs on the north side of Conachair (1,397 feet, 419 m) reach almost to the summit while on the western side the turreted buttresses of gabbro also rise a thousand feet (300 m) above the sea.

COASTAL LANDFORMS

The landforms along the coastline of the Highlands and Islands are both varied and of great value. They are the basis of some very fine scenery and a variety of economic activities. Much of the population of the Highlands and Islands is concentrated in the coastal zone where low angle slopes often combine with attractive superficial deposits to enable agriculture, settlement and routeway construction to take place.

The landforms that constitute the coast are the product of a wide range of processes acting under a variety of constraints. The actual form of the land where it meets the sea is the result of the interaction between various geomorphic processes and rock structures. The geomorphic processes may be related to the work of rivers or glaciers on the land area or to the work of waves in a zone between just below low water and just above high water. The zone of wave action will have changed with the passage of geological time, particularly during the Pleistocene when sea levels are believed to have fluctuated over 300 feet (90 m).

The factors affecting the development of coastal landforms may be divided into two broad groups. On the one hand, the orientation, shape and constituent material of the landforms as they come in contact with the sea determine the general shape of the coast. On the other hand the behaviour of the sea – in particular the size, shape and energy of the waves as they arrive at the coast – determine the efficiency of erosion and deposition in the coastal zone.

The overall shape of the coastline of the Highlands and Islands has been developed over a very long period of geological time. An examination of the charts of the off-shore zone around Scotland indicate that the present land mass is part of the continental shelf of Europe which terminates some 60 miles (100 km) west of the Outer Hebrides. All around the Highlands there are large areas of the sea

floor which are less than 300 feet (90 m) below sea level.
Information about the development of this off-shore zone is only
now being made available as a result of the exploration activities of
petroleum companies. There is still very little information available
about the recent history of the shallow seas around the Scottish
coasts.

The continental shelf to the west of the Highland mainland has
quite a complicated morphology. West of the Outer Hebrides there
is a gentle shelving to depths of 300 feet (90 m) to 600 feet (180 m)
before a rapid descent to over 5,000 feet (1,500 m). On the east side
of the Outer Hebrides there is a steep scarp, just off-shore, which
falls to depths between 300 feet (90 m) and 600 feet (180 m). This
scarp is believed to coincide with a tear fault which seems to have
displaced the metamorphic rocks forming the islands of the Outer
Hebrides in relation to similar rocks on the mainland. It is a matter
of debate whether activity along this fault line was responsible for
the flooding of this area by the sea to produce the Minch. The floor
of the Minch appears to contain a series of troughs which could be
explained as the continuation of river courses from the mainland
across the sea floor. These troughs can be linked with some of the
major valleys on the mainland west coat. Our knowledge of the
geology of the floor of the Minch is still very limited but it may well
have been invaded by the sea for a very long time.

Information about the history of the North Sea has been
provided in recent years as a result of exploration for oil and natural
gas. It appears that the North Sea basin has existed for hundreds of
millions of years and has been continuously and steadily infilled by
sediment derived from the erosion of surrounding land masses.
Except for the Norwegian trench, large areas of the North Sea are
only 200 feet (60 m) to 600 feet (180 m) deep. Again we know little
about the evolution of the surface form of the floor of the North
Sea.

It is perhaps tempting to explain the major outlines of the
Scottish coastline in terms of faulting on the margins of the North
Sea basin on the east and around the margins of the Minch in the
west. This may be justified in terms of the continuation of the Great
Glen fault along the north shore of the Moray Firth, in east
Sutherland and Caithness, but there is little evidence to support
such a statement on other parts of the coast. Once again, our lack of
knowledge of the events which took place during the Tertiary make
a full explanation of coastal landforms impossible. There is a lot of

evidence which suggests that the coastal forms are related to the pattern of preglacial river systems which were subsequently modified by the work of glaciers. Unfortunately there is no record of the sea level fluctuation which took place around the Scottish coast during the Tertiary.

The present coastline of the Highland mainland shows some marked contrasts between east and west. The west coast is generally backed by higher land and is much more indented than the east coast. It is fringed by many islands while the east coast has very few. The Outer Hebrides, incidentally, are almost a reversal of the mainland in as much their west sides are low and smooth while their east sides are often steep, rocky and indented.

Before examining the various types of coastal landforms around the Highlands and Islands it is necessary to discuss the processes currently at work along the coasts. The overall shape of the coastal zone has been shown to be the result of the geological history of the land area and its adjacent continental shelf. However, the detail forms immediately adjacent to present sea level are the result of the erosive and depositional work of waves. As wind moves across any body of water it generates waves on the water surface. When these waves reach shallow water they break and produce a lot of energy which can be used for erosion, transportation and deposition. Headlands being attacked by waves are eroded both by the very force of the water as well as by sand and shingle hurled against them. The eroded rock fragments are also transported by wave action into the heads of bays where they are deposited to form sand and shingle beaches. Not all the sand and shingle in beaches is produced by wave attack on cliffs. Some of it has been brought to the coast by rivers and glaciers where it has been re-worked by waves.

Over long periods of time wave attack along a coastline is capable of cutting a bench through solid rock at about sea level for a distance of several hundred yards to produce a wave-cut platform. Some of these platforms are partially buried by sand or shingle in their upper parts. The efficiency of wave erosion can be measured not only by the development of wave-cut platforms but by the development of caves in cliffs or by the occurrence of stacks – remnants of old cliffs standing beyond the present cliff line, indicating its former position.

The variety of coastal forms around the Highlands and Islands is so great that a detailed description of each part of the coastline is just not possible. What is possible is for me to describe five main types of coastline and to refer to some specific examples of each.

The west coast of the Highland mainland is mainly a fiord coast. That is, it consists of a series of glaciated valleys which have been invaded by the sea. Some of the fiords of the west coast are continued off-shore in the form of deep trenches below sea level. Such trenches occur in the Sound of Mull, the Firth of Lorne and between Rhum and Skye.

The classic fiord is a river valley which has had its sides steepened and floor deepened by the passage of glacier ice. Very often the floors of these valleys contain quite deep basins. The proximity of high ground near the west coast of the Highland mainland resulted in short steep valleys acting as routeways for glaciers on numerous occasions and these glaciers were fast flowing and vigorous. The common alignment of these valleys in certain areas suggests that their development was influenced by structures in the rocks in which they were cut. Many of the sea lochs in Sutherland are orientated south-east to north-west while many in the south-west Highlands are orientated from north-east to south-west. A great many of the west-coast fiords have deep basins in their central portions but become shallower near their mouths. Some of these

47.   Loch Hourn, fiord.

basins attain depths of several hundred feet (e.g. Loch Morar is 987 feet (296 m) deep). The rock lips at the lower end of some fiords are so close to present sea level that they act as water falls as the tide ebbs and flows (e.g. The Falls of Lora on Loch Etive). In other instances the lip is above present sea level (e.g. Loch Morar). Most of the fiords do not contain beaches of any size because their very sheltered character precludes any significant wave action. There is a wide range of form exhibited by the fiords of the west coast. Some are wide with relatively gentle side slopes e.g. Loch Fyne, while others are narrow and steep-sided e.g. Loch Hourn, (*Fig. 47*).

Since so much of the west coast is characterised by deep indentations, cliff formation and extensive sandy beaches have a limited distribution. Cliffs occur on headlands between the indentations and on islands. Cliffs over 100 feet (30 m) high occur at the south-western end of the Kintyre peninsula, in northern Jura, on the southern and northern coast of Mull, on the western coast of Rhum and on the western, northern and eastern coast of Skye. Very well-developed cliffs on Mull and Skye are related to Tertiary lavas.

There is only limited high cliff development in the Outer Hebrides but on the northern and eastern shores of the Highland mainland, cliffs occur along long stretches of coastline. They are particularly well-developed on Cambrian sediments and Moinian metamorphic rocks along the north coast of Sutherland and on sandstone on the north and south-east coast of Caithness. The most spectacular coastal scenery is found in the form of geos and stacks where resistant, gently-dipping beds – underlying a relatively high surface – are attacked by wave action along vertical joint planes. The sandstone cliffs at Dunnet Head are over 300 feet (90 m) high and the south-east coast of Caithness is cliffed along most of its length with the cliffs ranging between 50 feet (15 m) and 300 feet (90 m) in height.

Similar sandstone cliffs occur in Orkney. The gently dipping sandstones allow the development of almost vertical cliffs with numerous re-entrants. The long narrow openings known as 'geos' have resulted from weathering and erosion by the sea along faults, joints or dykes of igneous material. There are numerous examples along the west coast of the mainland. In many instances the landward end of a geo terminates in a cave, which further inland may be open to the surface through a 'gloup' or vertical chimney. The continued but slow retreat of the cliffs is demonstrated by the development of 'sea-stacks'. These pinnacles of rock were once attached to the cliff by an arch which collapsed, to produce the free standing pillars of rock. Sea-stacks result from the weathering and erosion along lines of weakness, probably faults or joints, in the original cliff. The most famous example is the Old Man of Hoy which stands 450 feet high. Magnificent cliffs are also developed on the exposed coasts of Unst, Yell, North Roe and the southern peninsula of the Mainland in the Shetlands. At Fitful Head, for example, the cliffs rise for nearly 900 feet (270 m) while on the west side of Foula they are over 1,000 feet (300 m) high.

There are large stretches of the coastline of the Highlands and Islands which are characterised by low rocky cliffs (less than 50 feet (15 m) high) and numerous small islands frequently referred to as skerries. This type of coastline is very characteristic of the north-west mainland (*Fig. 48*) and the eastern side of the Outer Hebrides and gives the impression that it results from the drowning by the sea of a coastal zone of very irregular surface form so that the coastline is characterised by great irregularity and many partially or completely drowned rock ridges.

Large sand and shingle beaches have a limited occurrence around the coastline of the Highlands and Islands. So much of the

48.   Skerry Coast.

west coast of the mainland is relatively well-protected that large accumulations of sand are rare, except on the western side of the Kintyre peninsula and the west coast of Sutherland. On the more exposed coasts of Islay, Mull and Skye and, more particularly, on the very exposed coasts of the west side of the Outer Hebrides extensive beaches have been developed. Around the shores of the Moray Firth there are also extensive beaches largely produced by the reworking of glacial and fluvioglacial deposits.

In the Orkney Islands, as well as some fine cliffs, there are also some excellent depositional forms. Essentially the Orkney coast-line has resulted from relatively recent submergence with Scapa Flow being the classical example of a basin being invaded by the sea to produce a very fine natural harbour. On exposed parts of the coast there are some excellent storm beaches as in Rackwick Bay on Hoy and linking Deerness to the mainland. These storm beaches are known locally as 'ayres'. In other locations a storm beach has grown across the entrance to a shallow bay or the mouth of a river and has produced a 'lake' such as the Peerie Sea at Kirkwall or Loch Tankerness behind the Long Ayre of Tankerness.

The smoothness of the west coast of the Outer Hebrides is in marked contrast to the crenellations of the east coast and is primarily the result of sand and shingle accumulation. Between rocky headlands there are wide sandy bays. Backed by dunes these, in turn, give way to an almost flat expanse of sand, frequently covered by grass and known as machair (*Fig. 49*). The sand forming the beaches, dunes and machair flats is a highly variable mixture of silicious and calcareous material. The silicious material is believed to have been derived from off-shore glacial deposits while the calcareous material is derived from crushed shells. The calcareous content can be as much as 60 per cent of the total and when it is present in significant amounts it allows the soils which develop on the machair to support a rich and varied flora and to be cultivated. The landforms created by these sand accumulations only extend inland for a distance of between half and one mile (0.8–1.6 km) and they only rarely attain heights greater than 50 feet (15 m) above sea level. It appears that most of the glacial material from which the sands and shingle were derived has already been brought on shore and most machair areas are no longer expanding. In some locations active erosion is taking place and 'blow-outs' occur, particularly in the dune areas. This is usually caused by over-grazing of the vegetation of the dunes or by removal of calcerous sands for use as a

49. Machair.

slow reacting liming material to reduce soil acidity in reseeding moorland areas. Although the finest examples of machair are to be found in the Outer Hebrides limited expanses occur on some of the more exposed coasts of the islands of the Inner Hebrides.

A great deal of the coastline of the Highland mainland and of the Inner Hebrides is characterised by fresh coastal forms such as rock platforms and beach deposits which are well above present sea level. These features relate to periods of relatively higher sea level which have occurred during the last 13,000 years. When Scotland was covered by a great ice sheet the weight of the ice was sufficient to depress the land surface and coastal forms were produced which, when the weight of the ice was removed, began to rise above sea level. Raised beaches and platforms up to 130 feet (40 m) above present sea level (*Fig. 50*) occur on the west Highland mainland and in the Inner Hebrides. Many of these features were formed as the ice of the last great ice sheet was melting away and they are often absent from the shores of many of the west-coast fiords, because they were still occupied by glaciers at the time of this relatively high sea level.

There was a delicate balance between the rate of the rise of the land as the ice sheet melted away and the rate of the rise of the sea as the meltwaters returned to the oceans. About 8,000 years ago sea level began to rise relative to the land and there was a marine transgression on to the land which culminated about 6,000 years

50. Raised marine platform, Islay.

51. Post-glacial raised-beach and abandoned cliff, Kintyre.

ago. This marine transgression produced a beach which at present is generally between 10 feet (3 m) and 40 feet (12 m) above present sea level in the south-west Highlands, Inner Hebrides and the Moray Firth. This shoreline is very well developed around the island of Arran, on Islay, in Kintyre (*Fig. 51*), and around the shores of the Sound of Jura. Both the late glacial and post glacial shorelines have been warped by the rebound of the land as a result of glacial unloading. In much of the older literature the Scottish raised beaches are described as '100 foot', '50 foot' or '25 foot'. This is incorrect, as a shoreline of any given age is at various altitudes depending upon the amount of rebound that has taken place. The greatest amount of rebound has taken place near the centre of the ice sheet which roughly coincided with the Moor of Rannoch. All the raised shorelines become progressively lower in altitude away from this central area. The Outer Hebrides and the Orkney and Shetland Islands do not have any raised shoreline features because they were so far away from the centre of ice accumulation that no rebound of the land has taken place. In both these areas, in fact, there is evidence to suggest that the sea level has risen relative to the land in post glacial times and that the coastline has been drowned. Further south, particularly in the Firth of Clyde, the southern and central sections of the west Highland mainland, the Inner Hebrides and around the Moray Firth the fact that sea level has fallen over the last 6,000 years means that there is often a coastal zone up to a mile (1.6 km) in width which contains landforms produced by marine erosion and deposition but which are no longer closely associated with present wave action. These older shoreline forms are of considerable significance in terms of land use patterns and in their effect upon the form and character of the present coastline.

Coastal landforms around the Highlands and Islands reflect the work of a specific set of geomorphological processes which have created particular environmental conditions. Early man arrived on these shores generally at a time when sea level was beginning to fall in the southern parts of the region. Since that time, the coastal landforms have played an important part in the economic development of the region, not least at present when not only the coast itself but the form of the submarine shelf is of great significance with the advent of off-shore exploration and exploitation of oil and natural gas.

LANDFORMS AS RESOURCES

The landforms of the Highlands and Islands vary greatly in character and in the part they play in the total natural environment. Each landform is made up of a series of slopes and of a certain type of material. In some ways the study of landforms can be regarded as the study of the distribution of slopes. For example, a valley consists of a series of valley-side slopes linked to valley-bottom slopes and a coastline consists of a series of land slopes truncated by sea level. In both cases each of the slopes has an inclination and plan shape and consists of either solid rock or unconsolidated sediments (e.g. sand and gravel). A very large percentage of the Highlands and Islands is made up of slopes with relatively steep gradients arranged in patterns which produce alternating valleys and ridges. This mountainous landscape occupies over 80 per cent of the region and gives it its very distinctive character. The 20 per cent of the region formed by low angle slopes, mostly in the form of valley bottoms and coastal lowlands, coincides with those areas most intensively used by man for agriculture and settlement sites.

The relationship between man's use of the land and landform in the Highlands and Islands is very marked. Low angle slopes combined with low altitude have always been the most attractive sites for human activity. In contrast, steep slopes and high altitude provide obstacles to human activity. The relationship between landforms and land use is not always direct as landforms also affect climate and vegetation which in turn affect land use. In very general terms the areas of high altitude in Scotland coincide with more extreme climatic conditions in that they experience lower winter temperatures, stronger winds and higher precipitation totals. The combination of landforms and climate also affect natural vegetation although in Scotland man has been responsible for altering the vegetation cover to a considerable extent. Over much of the Highlands trees once grew to 2,500 feet (750 m) above sea level but these were removed by man for fuel or to create grazing land for sheep. As a result heather moorland is now the predominant non-cultivated vegetation over most of the region.

One indication of the effect of landforms on man's use of the land is the measure known as relative relief, that is the difference in altitude between the highest and lowest altitudes in a given area (e.g. one kilometre square). The larger the value of relative relief the steeper the slopes and the lower the percentage of ground with low angle slopes. It must be pointed out that high values of relative relief do not always coincide with high absolute altitudes. For example, there are quite large areas on the Cairngorm plateau which have low relative relief values. However, if one examines two contrasting areas such as Ben Nevis and Caithness then it is easy to see how relative relief is a useful expression of the character of the landforms. In the Ben Nevis area relative relief values of between 1,200 feet (360 m) and 1,800 feet (540 m) per square kilometre are quite common whereas in Caithness relative relief values of between 50 feet (15 m) and 250 feet (75 m) per square kilometre are common.

One further variable has to be added to altitude and relative relief before the effect of landforms on land use can be studied. Landforms consist of a wide variety of materials and it is especially important to distinguish between those landforms consisting of solid rock and those consisting of unconsolidated materials such as clay, sand or gravel. Large areas of the Highlands and Islands consist of solid rock with no cover of unconsolidated material. In those areas the actual character of the solid rock is very important. If the landforms consist of hard resistant material like the gneiss of Harris, Lewis and much of western Sutherland they will be quite different from those consisting of less resistant sandstone, as in Caithness. In other areas the solid rock has a cover of unconsolidated material and it is this cover which provides the details of the landforms upon which human activity takes place. The nature of the material constituting landforms in any area is largely a reflection of the geological history of that area.

The land of the Highlands and Islands is a great natural resource and the form of that land plays an important part in determining its use by man. The distribution of population within the region is closely correlated with the distribution of low angle slopes. The present population of the region is concentrated either on coastal lowlands or on valley floors. It is possible, in fact, to go even further and note that the largest rural population is associated with areas either of relatively young consolidated sedimentary rocks, e.g. the Old Red Sandstone sediments of Caithness and Easter Ross and Cromarty, or of very recent unconsolidated sediments, e.g. the machair sands of the Outer Hebrides or the fluvioglacial sands and gravels of the valley floors throughout the region.

The relationship between population distribution and landform type also reflects the type of land use upon which the population is dependent. The various types of agricultural activity found in the Highlands depend largely on landform distribution. Arable cultivation is certainly limited to low angle slopes and low altitude whereas the more extensive activities of sheep and cattle grazing are associated with the higher land and with steep slopes. Much of the better grazing land is also suitable for forestry and hence the debate about the value of reafforestation of this type of land.

The establishment of nucleated settlements in the Highlands and Islands can also be related to the distribution of landforms in three ways. Firstly, the availability of actual sites with suitable low angle slopes again means that settlements are concentrated on valley floors and on coastal sites. The occurrence of a narrow zone of flat land around much of the coast of the Highlands and Islands is a direct result of geological events of the recent past and it is not surprising that many settlements and routeways have taken advantage of this zone of low angle slopes. The nature of the Scottish coastline can be summarised by one word: indented. The reasons for the many indentations have already been discussed but, from the point of view of the economic activities upon which the population depend then these indentations often provide sheltered and deep water harbours on which fishing fleets are based. During the wars and in recent years, the advantages of these deep inlets both for defence and the construction of oil platforms has brought developments which would not have taken place were it not for this unique relationship between land and sea.

The form of the off-shore zone has been of great importance in the past in that the occurrence of shallow shelf-seas around the Highlands and Islands has been the basis of a very important fishing industry. In more recent years it has been discovered that the great sedimentary basin which underlies the North Sea is a potential source of large quantities of oil and natural gas. The North Sea has been a sedimentary basin for many millions of years and particularly during the Tertiary some 3,000 m of sediment – some of it derived by the erosion of the Scottish Highlands – accumulated in the basin. It is in these and older sediments that the oil and natural gas occurs. It is only possible to gain access to these resources because much of the floor of the North Sea is only 200 feet (60 m) to 600 feet (180 m) below present sea level. Fortuitous, indeed, that these vital resources occur beneath a shallow shelf sea in which present levels of technology allow exploration and exploitation! It is also fortuitous that around the western and northern shores of the Highlands, there are deep fiords which are suitable for the construction and floatation of the platforms required to exploit the deposits on the floor of the North Sea.

Another way in which the landforms of the Highlands and Islands have contributed directly to their economic development has been the provision of suitable conditions for the generation of hydroelectricity. Large areas of high altitude and steep slopes in the path of the westerly moist airstream from the Atlantic result in heavy precipitation. This water can be stored by the construction of dams across narrow deep valleys. The water from these reservoirs is carried by pipes to locations with high relative relief values to provide a good head of water for power generation. The North of Scotland Hydro-electric Board now has an output capacity of 1,752 megawatts of power from fifty-six stations throughout this area.

The landforms of the Highlands and Islands can also be regarded as a major resource simply because they provide some of the most attractive scenery in western Europe. Not only the mountainous scenery of the north-west but also the wide straths of the east and also the magnificent coastal scenery of both the mainland and the islands attract a great many tourists and bring a large income into the region. The value of landforms as scenery is difficult to measure but as the rest of Europe becomes increasingly urbanised the pressures on this resource become even greater. For many tourists, simply to drive through attractive landscape is satisfying enough. To the more adventurous, the pleasure derived from walking over the landforms and discovering the more remote parts is considerable. To the mountaineer, the landforms of higher altitudes with their rock faces present an even greater challenge and in some cases considerable danger. To the scientist, the landforms of this region have provided the evidence upon which to build theories of the history and evolution of landforms which are applicable to areas far beyond Scotland. The landforms of the Highlands and Islands are a very important part of the natural environment. They constitute the surface upon which human activity takes place and can be regarded as an important natural resource in their own right. They play an important part in influencing a wide variety of economic activities and both directly and indirectly influence the distribution of population within the region.

SELECTED REFERENCES

D. Brunsden and J. C. Doornkamp: The Unquiet Landscape, London 1972.
G. Y. Craig: The Geology of Scotland, Edinburgh 1983.
A. Geikie: The Scenery of Scotland, London 1901.
J. Geikie: The Great Ice Age, London 1894.
G. S. Johnstone: The Grampian Highlands: British Regional Geology; Institute of Geological Sciences; HMSO 1966.
J. Phemister: The Northern Highlands: British Regional Geology; Institute of Geological Sciences, HMSO 1960.
R. J. Price: Glacial and Fluvioglacial Landforms, Edinburgh 1973 and London 1976.
R. J. Price: Scotland's Environment during the last 30,000 years, Edinburgh 1983.
J. E. Richey: The Tertiary Volcanic Districts; British Regional Geology; Institute of Geological Sciences; HMSO 1962.
J. B. Sissons: The Evolution of Scotland's Scenery; Edinburgh 1967.
J. B. Sissons   Scotland (The Geomorphology of the British Isles), London 1976.
B. W. Sparks and R. G. West: The Ice Age in Britain; London 1972.
J. A. Steers: The Coastline of Scotland; Cambridge 1973.

Maps: The landforms and geology of the Highlands and Islands are well illustrated by maps produced at a variety of scales by the Ordnance Survey and the British Geological Survey.

INDEX